TH

Player

THE DIARY OF A *Player*

MATTHIAS BRAY

The Diary of a Player

Oct 15, 2016
First Paperback Edition

ISBN 978-0-9826175-2-6
Pearl Publishing, LLC
2587 Southside Blvd, Melba, ID 83641
http://pearlpublishing.net—1.888.499.9666

Contents

Foreword

Why in the world, one might ask, would a Player write a book about himself and uncover his secret world of seduction and deception?

Perhaps it is the same search for redemption that criminals possess when they leave clues behind at the crime scene—hoping one day they will be caught because they are not strong enough to stop their actions on their own. And not being able to live a fulfilling life because of their crimes, they seek to end their self-castigation by hoping that one day society will catch them and punish them for what they have done.

Are crimes of the heart any less criminal in nature than crimes against society? Do the perpetrators use the same means to commit offenses against their unknowing victims? Does their reasoning and justification of such crimes parallel the criminal mindset? Then again, maybe there's no such thing as a "crime of the heart." Human beings create the laws that make actions become "crimes," so perhaps they also accept deceptive, manipulative, and purposeful actions against the heart as a *normal* part of human behavior.

When does a society have a right to stand up and punish one of its members for hurting another person? Are not crimes of the heart just as real, and do they not hurt just as much as criminal offenses against a person or property? Wisdom should determine which laws are necessary in order to maintain a peaceful environment for society. Yet it can be proven that many "real" crimes are committed as a reaction to a crime that was committed against a heart.

How many homes and families have been broken because of these un-punishable misdeeds? How many women have turned to drugs and alcohol to soothe the tightened pulsations of their broken hearts? How many others have turned to food as the permanent replacement for self-control because they will never be controlled or manipulated by a man again?

A Player is a criminal. His actions are crimes that affect society in many subtle, but devastating ways. He plays women for his own self-gratification and to boost his own self-esteem. His victims are chosen wisely and carefully, using premeditation in each instance. Soon his crimes become second nature, and his illusory nature becomes the only reality that he knows and understands.

If a society is to place blame on these types of emotional predators, then it is only just that it attempts to also understand them. To make a righteous judgment that can result in a just punishment, a degree of understanding and compassion must be present in order to maintain a modern civility and respect for personal freedom.

The Diary of a Player is real. The situations presented in the book are indeed a reflection of true human nature and give a real presentation of the emotional problems associated with *real* players. The book was written to help others understand who a player is and why they are this way. The author wanted to warn unaware victims of the type of nature players have, and the methods they use to seduce and manipulate women for their own needs. There are thousands of Players in society taking advantage of "the game" that they play so well. The author knows that all men are capable of becoming a Player. It is his hope that these types of men will gain a better understanding of their own intentions toward women and that women will be made aware of these types of men as they read what they are all about.

The worst thing a reader could say to him or herself is, "Oh, this is not me or my partner. My man is different." Closing one's mind to a possibility makes a probability more likely to occur. Read this book with an open mind and a desire to understand and learn. It will open your eyes, your heart, and your mind to a realm of reality that most people do not want to face—the reality of human nature.

—Editor

Self-Realization

"Who am I?" I often ask myself each morning as I look into the bathroom mirror.

My bluish-green eyes seem to sparkle in the light of the six 40-watt bulbs that illuminate the meticulous bathroom that I allow no one but myself to clean. My strong chin and cut face shine in the mirror that reflects an image that I don't understand, and sometimes hate.

Now don't get me wrong, I am attractive, and my body is one that other 35-year-old men wish they had. And my personality—what can I say—it is one that exudes the hidden fantasies of most women. Yes, I must say, I know what to say, what to do, and how to do it to get any woman I set my sights on. Admittedly, I am not a pretty boy, but with my personality traits, the heart and soul of any woman is mine for the taking. The epitome of what a woman wants—Yep, that's me!

Maybe that's why I sometimes hate what I see in the mirror. There, looking back at me is the deceiver, the liar, the manipulator who preys on the innocence and trust of women. A man who knows what he has to do to get sex from his unaware victims whose hearts are served to him on a silver platter of codependency that I call LOVE.

But the women love me. They say that I am the best thing that ever happened to them. They rave at the fact that they have found one of the only truly "nice" guys left. They tell me that I kiss good, make love incredibly, and know how to treat a woman. They like the gentle way that I caress their hair and their faces. They cherish the sweet way that I speak to them and tell them that they are special and "one-of-a-kind." They like it when I tell them that there is much more to them than their incredible bodies and lips. They like the idea that I am intelligent and have a character unmatched by most of the men they have dated. They love my smile, my humor, my love and compassion for others. But mostly, they love the way that I treat them.

But who do they really love?

Who am I? Am I genuinely sincere in what I tell these women? Do I really feel a passion for them when I treat them like a queen? Or is it I that need the attention, the affection, the reassurance that I am wanted and loved? Are my actions towards them merely coercive enticements to make them want me? Does the passion that they feel toward me settle the uneasiness that I feel inside—the anxiety, the mistrust, and the pain? Does deceiving them bring power to a powerless heart that is scared and alone? I make them believe that they are needed until they truly need me. Then the prey is caught, the life sucked out of an open heart; and I devour the flowing trust that escapes the severed veins of their hearts. Then I feel powerful. I feel nourished. I feel in control. I feel like a man.

As I peer silently into the eyes looking back at me in the mirror, for a moment I catch a glimpse of a little boy—one who constantly fought for the attention of his young mother. She dashes across my memory, and I catch her in a moment of time that seems endless:

A tiny baby boy born to a 20-year-old mother who already had two brothers waiting for him—one 3 years old and the other only 1. The baby boy clings tightly to her, and yearns for the tender affection that only a mother can give. To add insult to his unquenched desire for affection, his mother presents him with a baby brother exactly one year, one month and one day after his birth. A year later, a sister is born.

Middle child syndrome.

Is there such a thing? Or is it fate's design? There, between a 5 year-old, a 3 year-old, a 1 year-old, and a newborn baby girl, fate placed him, and dealt a hand to this affectionate, clingy, and needy 2 year-old boy that would affect his life forever. But fate hadn't played all her cards yet. The dashing mother disappears from my view, and I remember very little more about her. Yet, in those eyes in the mirror I see that little boy running after her, chasing her, searching for the only one that could calm his anxieties. But she is gone, and no one is there to replace her.

A tear runs down my sculpted cheek and falls gently into the porcelain sink, then finds its way to the drain, where it disappears without making a sound. There go my emotions. Is this how a woman is supposed to treat a man? Bring him into this life totally dependent on her in every way and then leave him? It won't happen again. Before they leave me and take away their affection, I will leave them—wanting me, aching for me, and feeling what they deserve.

Maybe it wasn't my childhood experiences that made me who I am today. Maybe it was nature. Throughout the whole of the animal kingdom, males entice the females to want them and mate with them.

When the mating is over, the enticing and promenade to sex starts again. The peacock shows off his brilliant colors, the frog forces romantic gestures of passion from deep within his throat, the grouse fluffs his feathers and beats the ground in hopes that his dance is recognized first above all other suitors—all in hopes that each can end their charade in sex.

Are human males any different? Or have we developed different, yet similar techniques through emotional and physical evolution that win a woman's heart and feed on her codependency? (Oh, there's that word! The word that defines love.) Do we not strut our stuff, show our feathers, and croak our passions in hopes that we can entice a woman to sleep with us? Some of us entangle our horns, bash our heads, and physically compete for a woman's attention. Some of us are more patient and subdued in our approach. We wait and stalk and do what we know the woman wants, until we realize we have won the prize of her affection. Then we pounce on her and consummate our claim. Some of us are satisfied to win a prize and proudly display it on our mantle for all other males to see and envy. Thus the ring—the symbol of our ownership and possession that wards off the desires of other suitors. But does the dance stop there? No it does not. We are not made that way. We have our trophy, but desire to believe that we can still "strut our stuff" and take a female if we wanted. And do we want another female, besides our trophy? You bet we do! Any man that says he doesn't is a liar and denying what his biological urges force him to admit.

Strutting our stuff. How we do it? Why do we do it? Has it ever crossed a woman's mind that the stuff that we strut is not really who we are? Of course it is not. It is what the woman wants us to be. I can be anything a woman wants me to be if I want her bad enough. I'll pretend to like cats and dogs, children, bicycle rides and long romantic walks on the beach. I'll pretend I like to look at photos of her family and share old memories of what it was like to be in High School. I'll pretend to care about her disabled brother and ailing mother, her weird uncle, or famous cousin. I'll tell her that her dress looks great on her, when I really don't care what covers the object of my intention. Yes, I will be the perfect man; until, of course, we've had sex and she is mine. Once I have her committed and dedicated only to me, then I can start showing her who I really am.

The mirror has created the dilemma. As I look at the two dimensional refractions of light rays as colors, what do they really mean? Who am I? Maybe I don't want to know. Maybe I want others to never know, and that is why I become to others what they want to see. Maybe I am afraid of knowing who I really am and only want to know what others see. Yes, that's it! I only want to know myself as others know me. I can control this. I can become whoever I want to be. Because I am a man, a Player—a handsome, charismatic, and debonair connoisseur of male cuisine that makes women salivate and drown in their own drool. They should have swallowed the saliva or spit it out, but they couldn't—it was too good, too enticing, so they drowned themselves in it. I am not to blame. I am innocent, untarnished, and unstained. I gave them what they wanted and took what I deserved. I am a man.

I am a good man—different from the rest. I care more about what I can give to a relationship than I do about what I get out of it. I have looked long and hard for the perfect woman and I have finally found her. She means everything to me, and I want no other. Though I am in love with her, I am afraid of commitment because of past hurt that I have to deal with every day. Not able to make a commitment, because of my fear of losing love again, I lay my heart out for the right woman to find, hold, and heal. The right woman found me and with her natural desire to nurture, she became my healer, my confidant, my lover…

…At least that's what three different women think. All of them think they are the only one for me. Each is in love with the image that I have created and personalized especially for her. Each is unaware of the other and believes in her heart that I could not possibly love anyone but her. Each is deceived, lied to, and manipulated—treated exactly and sincerely like I am. Maybe that is why they believe me, because I am sincere. They are totally unaware that the hurt I am referring to when I explain my inability to commit doesn't exist consciously. Perhaps it exists subconsciously, somewhere between my longing for my mother and running after her. I lie to them, making them think that I am hurt—in need of their healing touch because some other woman broke my heart.

Women are suckers for guys they think have been hurt by someone else. The hurt that they assume I am referring to is the hurt of a woman who I loved with all my heart, but she left me for another man. I make them believe that I was hopelessly in love with this surreal woman, thus giving them the impression that when I fall in love, I do so deeply, monogamously and completely. I convince them that

I have left the dating arena and have been with none other, until I found the sucker that is falling for this bullshit story.

So maybe that's who I am. If I have found myself in that image in the mirror, then I can accept me for me and be who I really am, undaunted by the thought that I might be someone that I can't see. I am satisfied with who I am and love myself. Yep, I truly am a man!

With this daily ritual, I start my morning. With the final realization of who I am, I can begin to shape the outward appearance to conform with the image of the "real" me.

The shower comes first. I begin by washing my hair, thankful that at my age I still have a full head of soft hair that brings delight to any woman that finds her fingers allowed to touch it. I grab a clean washcloth, cover it with soap, and dig it deep into my face to extract any residue of dirt that might hide my manly appearance. More importantly, it's vital that any lingering smell of the woman I just slept with is removed. I move the washcloth along my sculptured chest that is covered with just the right amount of hair, not too little, and not too much.

Ah, yes! The chest. A woman's delight if sculpted just right, and presented in a way that lets her know that I take little notice in her desire to touch it. If presented too presumptuously, the intent is foiled by her defense mechanism that has taught her to pull away from any man who is in love with himself.

I drape the washcloth neatly over the shower door and with soap in hand continue to clean the rest of my body. My hands smooth over the hairline on my chest that guides them to my stomach. My stomach has no excess weight, is not as sculpted as I would like, but is probably a plus instead of the washboard "ab look," which would be a definite giveaway that I am too concerned about my physical appearance.

It's obvious women do not like a man who is stuck on himself, but they do love hard bodies that are athletic and defined. Of course, when asked if I workout, the answer is always humbly, "Sometimes, but not as often as I probably should." Again maintaining the façade that I am not too possessed with my physical appearance, when in reality it is one of the biggest selling points of sex.

I pause for a moment, and wonder if that's what it is. Could it be that the face in the mirror was good-looking enough its entire life, that its owner expected females to want him as they always have. Since he was a little boy hearing others comment on what a handsome boy he is, to a grown man who notices the glances of women as he walks into a room. Could it be possible that my looks have gained me so much attention that the thought of only getting that attention from one woman makes me insecure and uneasy?

I have always heard that in order for a man to be truly happy he should marry a woman uglier than himself. This wasn't hard for me; and looking back, it was easy to see why I had so few stunning girlfriends. Perhaps I was afraid they wouldn't give me the attention I needed, so I avoided them. Real good-looking girls don't need to give attention—they get it all. The same with real good-looking men. I used my looks to entice, and my learned "strutting" to conquer. I need to conquer, so I am forced to entice. I am thankful for my looks and my body.

Perhaps it was the fact that I excelled in athletics. The girls wanted me and the guys envied me. In college I had two girlfriends, and only limited myself to two because it was harder to be a player when I was taking 20 credit hours and playing football. Of course, I chose the two best looking, naïve girls I could find. (However, they thought I considered each of them the brightest girl on campus.) These types wanted my body as much as I wanted theirs, but were easily manipulated and lied to. But all women can be manipulated and lied to, no matter how intelligent they think they are. A good player can get anyone he wants. It just takes more time and patience to get the smarter ones. Anyway, I received accolades on and off the field from many people. I got used to the attention. It became a big part of who I am—a player on and off the field.

Before the bar of soap reaches the area of the groin where all men's fantasies are played out on a stage of hope, need, and expectation, my soapy hand finds my buttocks—another enticement to the female species. Women like nice asses. I fondle my buttocks a little, gentle squeezing each cheek to feel if it has substance. Doing so turns me on a bit with the fantasy thought of how much a woman would enjoy doing the same thing. Briefly my mind escapes to some of the great asses I have touched. I love a firm butt. I don't mind bigger butts, in fact, at times, they're the best, but it must be firm and shaped proportionately. Reaching for a woman's ass during intercourse and holding it in my hand comes only second to watching a woman cum. To watch a woman with a sculpted butt seductively undress, drives all men absolutely crazy.

The bar of soap finally reaches my groin area and begins to clean the weapon of choice in a man's pursuit and eventual conquest of a woman. There in my hand I hold one of the only differences between a man and woman. Maybe this is why we often fantasize about our woman sleeping with another woman and doing it in front of us. We are not threatened by this act, because neither participant has what we have—a firm, natural penis. Oh, but if another man were to introduce his weapon, it would be a battle to the death.

Yes, men protect their penises and the object of the penis' use more than anything else they own. We stand in bathrooms pissing trying to inconspicuously glance at the weapons of other men to see how ours compare. We've all done it. We all want to know if our weapons are as big and as powerful as the next guy's. By God, (pun intended), we even come up with religions to protect our proud penises and the way they are used.

The Law of Moses in the Bible is a definite protector of the male right to wield his sword when and how he wants. If a man lie with a woman and she is not betrothed to another man, then the man is justified in doing so, no matter how forceful, as long as he takes the woman to be his wife. Now, it doesn't matter if the man is already married, he can have as many wives as he pleases. But God forbid that a woman who is married should sleep with another man. If she does, she is instantly stoned to death. The man is the head of the woman, Adam was created first, God is a man—it doesn't take a rocket scientist to figure out that most of the religions of the world were created by men, for men, and because of men.

Hell, the Muslims believe that this guy named Mohammed was inspired to go into the wilderness searching for the true God and find the true way. He eventually hooked up with Allah who came to him and called him to be the prophet of the last dispensation of time. Allah told Mohammed that all the other religions were false, and that he would organize the belief system that held all the keys to the mysteries of heaven. The prophet Mohammed took his job seriously and started his new religion. He then wrote a book (The Koran) and quickly introduced polygamy as a righteous act that one needed to do to please Allah. In the early 1800's a guy named Joseph Smith (prophet of the Mormons) went through about the same scenario, and many of his male followers get the privilege of sleeping with many wives under the justification that God is pleased. Yea, God is pleased! God is man, and man is God. Thank God I am a man!

By now, my penis has grown fairly long and hard as the soap washes off the residue of the woman I slept with last night. The dried cum slowly and quietly disappears down the same drain system that my tear fell down moments before. There go my emotions once again. But, oh, holding the essence of my manliness brings me a sense of power and control. How many women have I slept with in my life? A hundred, two hundred, a thousand? I don't even remember. All I have to worry about are the three I am sleeping with presently. I have control over these naïve pussies who are so easily deceived and manipulated by my weapon.

My soapy hand finds the testicles that hang hard and low below their master and king. Each one filled with the potential of life now lay dormant, having the stream of life interrupted by the snip of a surgeon's scissors. This gives me control over my weapon even more. I can shoot it off as often as I want, at whatever target I want, without worrying about my aim causing me any unwanted responsibility. I hold them tenderly for a moment thinking about their potential and power. Ahhhh, I am glad I am a man.

I begin to gently stroke myself finding my ability to turn myself on also very powerful. The strokes get harder and harder as the weapon that my hand is around becomes harder and harder. The warm water from the shower simulates the warm cum of a woman, and my heart rate increases with each stroke. Suddenly I realize that I have to save myself for the upcoming day—I have two different women who want me inside of them today. Again, I am amazed at the control that I have over my weapon and gently put it down, clean, fresh, and ready to shoot again.

Dripping wet, I reach for the clean towel closest to me. I wipe the beads of water from my body and shake the excess water from my hair. Once again I find myself looking in the mirror, usually in adoration. I take a step back and flex my chest muscles in unison with the whistle that I use to let a woman know I think she is hot. They bounce magically in rhythm with the whistle. Stepping a little further back, I stand on my tiptoes, turn to the side, and flex my butt cheek to assure that it doesn't look flabby or full of "cottage cheese" marks. Satisfied, I turn the other way inspecting its twin. "Not perfect, but acceptable," I proclaim.

I grab the blow dryer and force out the remaining moisture in my hair, carefully maneuvering the hot air so that it sets my hair where it needs to be. When I have it in place, I admire its handsome manifestation and recall the countless women who have run their fingers through it, wondering if it belonged to "their man." I get turned on again as I recall the many hands that have grasped it during intercourse and forcefully drawn my head to the parts of their bodies that women long for a man to kiss, lick, and caress with his lips and tongue.

My penis gets hard again, so I end the thoughts with a deep smile that resonates with satisfaction that I am wanted and needed.

Again, my mind wanders back to my childhood. I sucked my thumb and twirled that hair of mine until I was seven years old. Maybe I am a bit obsessed with my hair because it was my security blanket—my distraction from the reality that I didn't have my mother's hair to play with. From seven years old on, all I can remember is that hair of mine being pulled when I did something wrong—when I acted out to get attention. Damn this hair, I hate it! If women didn't like it, I would shave it all off! But they do, so I need it.

Dress for Success

A man's smell is vital to who he is and how a woman remembers him. My smell is unique to me, and one that has brought me considerable success with my women. Too much cologne or after-shave is repulsive and usually indicates that the man has something to hide. It's like chewing gum all the time. Any woman that constantly chews gum, obviously has bad breath she is hiding, so I usually avoid excessive gum chewers.

The right cologne placed in the right places on a man's body will drive women wild. What's the best way to figure out where to put it? Why ask a woman, of course! The countless women that I have been with have all contributed to my understanding of personal hygiene. Since I deceive them in so many other ways, I figure telling them that I am an incompetent dresser and that I don't usually wear cologne, but would like to for them, is justified and productive.

Women like to dress men. Most of my wardrobe consists of a woman's desire to dress "her man" properly. I haven't bought a new shirt, pants, or tie in years. Thanks, my broken-hearted sugar mamas!

I guess I like women to dress me, at least I love that they want to, and I take advantage of their desire to be a nurturing mother. Yea, I guess I need them to.

The rest of my personal hygiene is accomplished without much fanfare or thought. I brush my teeth, shave, pick out any excess nose hair, ear hair, and any other hair that stands out. That's one thing men hate about women—excess nose hair. What a turn-off to get close to a woman, look at her nose, and see some straggling hair protruding out her nostril. Another gripe and total turn-off are the women who take to shaving to remove the hair on their face. Nothing turns me off more than to kiss a woman and feel stubble. If she has a nice ass or great tits, she might get to fuck me a few times, but ultimately I will lose interest a lot sooner than my usual loss-of-interest time frame, if I feel like I am kissing a man. Anyway, I finish my outward façade and head for the closet.

In my closet, one will find all my shirts, sweaters, pants, suits, and ties. Each is hung neatly and clean, ready for its next adventure. As I enter the closet to choose my wardrobe, my thoughts begin racing through the tentative events of the day. A Player has got to have a fast, clear, and sharp mind. Each thought, each lie, each manipulation must be anticipated, timed, and seem as if it were thoughtless. What am I going to wear to work? Who will see me there? When will I see the first? The second? Possibly the third? Has she seen me in these clothes before? And if she hasn't, what kind of story am I going to come with as to how I got this shirt, this tie, and these shoes?

"God, I can't wear that pair of leather shoes!" I startled myself.

Amy had given them to me yesterday because I had mentioned how much I love leather and the way my feet breathe with it. Two days previous to receiving my gift from Amy, I had taken Victoria shopping to buy her a pair of shoes for her birthday. In the shoe store, I analytically explained how leather can irritate the feet and lose its flexibility after getting wet. I was dissuading her from buying the more expensive leather shoes, and convinced her that I cared about her comfort, and that the new synthetic materials, which by the way are much, much cheaper, were scientifically designed to conform to modern-day usage. I explained that it was a shame that we had to take the hides from innocent animals (showing my animal rights side—women love a man that loves animals) to satisfy our fashion lusts.

I am going to see Victoria after work today, and surely she will notice the brand new, expensive leather shoes that I have on. However, I'll be seeing Amy also today for lunch, and she might wonder why I am not wearing the gift she had given me.

As quickly as these thoughts enter my mind, my genius comes through in microseconds, and I realize that I can wear the leather shoes to work and take another pair with me for after work. I can put the leather shoes away in the trunk of my car before I go see Victoria. And if by some chance I happen to open the trunk and Victoria sees the leather shoes, they're new, so I can easily say that my aunt had given them to me for my birthday a couple of years ago. So not wanting to upset her, I kept them, and had forgotten that I had thrown them in my trunk in case I ever went to see her. (The aunt excuse works great. What's even better is if you have a liberal aunt that loves you, knows you're a player, and covers for you. If you have such a one, you're covered. Having friends that cover for you, especially female friends, is one of the greatest assets a Player could have.)

With the shoe problem out of the way, I chose a neutral pair of pants, a shirt, and a tie I had before I met the present women in my life. Since the average time I spend with each is about 4 to 6 months, I don't concern myself too much about them worrying about the wardrobe that I bring into the relationship, and end up throwing a lot of great clothes away just so I can make the women feel good about buying me something. Each time one of them buys me something I always tell her that I have never received a gift from a woman before, and that I feel so special for receiving hers. I like to get gifts.

Maybe my birthdays were the best days of my life. These were my special days. My family and friends acknowledged me and brought me gifts. It didn't matter if I acted spoiled on these days; it was my birthday. On these special days my father would smile at me more often, even my step-mom would step out of her norm and treat me a little like her own flesh and blood. Even my brothers and sisters would treat me a little better than on a regular day. I miss those birthdays. To hell with those childhood satisfactions, I can have a birthday and a special day of attention every time I get involved with a new woman. Yes, I love getting gifts.

The Crime Scene

Dressed and ready for work, I head out the door of my small, comfortable apartment. Breakfast usually consists of a yogurt and a muffin or piece of bread. A Player doesn't need to cook; if he does, it is only to impress a new woman with his eclectic talents and feminine side. Nothing impresses a woman more, and probably has the highest success rating for getting fucked on the first date, than a home-cooked meal in a handsome man's comfortable, little apartment.

Men don't have to worry much about knowing how to cook. Pasta rules. You can do all kinds of things with pasta, and it is usually served with a nice white wine that aids in the seducing process. Pasta is quick and easy. I only know of three meals that I can cook without uncovering the fact that I don't know how, nor do I care to learn: spaghetti with a tomato sauce (the sauce can vary); pasta with cream sauce, served with shrimp; and angel hair pasta with a light vinaigrette.

If a woman has sampled all three of my specialties, it usually means that she is one of the cautious ones who has set definite rules about how many times she'll date a man before she sleeps with him. A good Player can spot these types right away, and usually needs a few home-cooked meals to get her ready.

No woman as of yet has ever tasted all three of my home-cooked specialties.

I mentioned leaving my small, comfortable apartment for work. A Player's residence is essential to his ability to win the hearts and trust of his women. The most desirable abode is one shared with another Player who knows the game and loves to play it as much as his roommate. However, since each Player is different in his approach, most pads are different in their appearance. You don't want too big of an apartment. Keep it small, yet clean and comfortable. Make sure the kitchen is very small and inconvenient—the bathrooms too. There is great wisdom in this. Women love spacious houses and big kitchens and bathrooms. Therefore, if they see how inconvenient yours is, they are more likely to invite you over to their house.

One of the greatest strategies of a Player is to keep his women out of his home as much as possible, always have a home phone number and a cell phone—never a pager—and never accept any of their personal photos. Women love to give their man a photo of themselves. Yet, how is a man going to justify not having it proudly displayed at his bedside or fireplace mantle when the hopeless romantic drops by for a surprise visit?

Herein lies one of the biggest problems for the Player—the unexpected visit. You have to assure that the women hate coming over to your house, so that they don't drop by to surprise you. Nevertheless, inevitably it will happen, that's why I never park my car in the same parking space when I come home. If one drops by unexpectedly, I don't have to answer the door and she won't see my car. If by some chance she happens to drive by my car parked a distance from its assigned parking space, it can easily be explained away by telling her that I had to lend the car to a neighbor whose wife was ill and whose car was in the shop. Women love compassionate hearts.

Back to the "Here, honey I want you to have this photo of me." I tell them that I hate photos because it makes me miss them too much. I explain that I would rather have the 3-dimensional reality in front of me, than a 2-dimensional fantasy. Without a photo, I am more inclined to want to see her again when I am away. I explain that a photo can never do her beauty the justice it deserves. And if all that bullshit doesn't convince her, I get teary-eyed and explain that I have developed a phobia of photos ever since my mother left me as a small boy and only left a photo as a memory—a photo that I can't bear to look at even for a moment without painful memories of her loss. That works every time, and usually ends in a warm embrace, some necking, and a sympathetic fuck from a woman who wants to take my pain away. Maybe, the woman isn't as manipulated as I think she is. Maybe the mother story is told so sincerely and realistically that she senses the truth of it. I hate photos anyway.

Never, never allow any woman's clothing or jewelry to be left in your apartment. One time I had sex with a gorgeous waitress who was just getting off work, and had a fight with her boyfriend on the phone, who had ended up telling her to walk home. I had just paid my check and watched the poor thing leave in tears. It didn't take much of my charm to convince her that my warm car would be a lot better than an 8-mile walk. It took a little more charm to convince her that I was a great listener who lived close by and could make a great cup of hot chocolate. (You never want to offer an alcoholic beverage to a strange woman you meet—she'll become suspicious of your intent. Hot chocolate is more reminiscent of family and home.) She took the bait after I convinced her to let her boyfriend cool down a bit and maybe make him worry a little about her when she didn't show up until early in the morning.

I brought her home, listened to her tell her story about her unfeeling boyfriend, and gently hugged her telling her I understood and was sorry that there were so many men that didn't know how to treat a woman. I told her to give her boyfriend a chance, that he was probably insecure and unsure of himself like a lot of "us" men are. She was enchanted by my desire for her to work things out with her boyfriend, and quickly became comfortable and trusting in my small, warm apartment. I excused myself for a moment telling her I had left something in my car. Of course, my purpose was to go to my car and call Marlee, Number Three at the time, and tell her that I was on my way home and must have got some kind of food poisoning from something I ate, and that I would have to cancel our plans tonight. She was insistent on taking care of me, but I insisted that I be left alone so that I could sleep. I told her that I would never get the rest I needed as long as her gorgeous body was around to entice me—no matter how deathly ill I was.

I went back inside my apartment and found my sweet waitress mesmerized by the many books that adorned my bookshelf.

Ah, the bookshelf—another specialized tool in the enchantment process. Luckily, I was as well read as the books professed. Nietzsche, Plato, Einstein, Stephen Hawkins—each author speaks highly of my ability to think and attempt to understand life and the human soul. Women love a deep thinker. I can carry on a conversation as simple as how pets comfort old people to quantum physics. Do I understand it all? Not entirely. But to a novice in any field, I can usually appear equal or beyond. When I meet a woman that is an expert in a particular field, I present myself as humble, enthusiastic, and eager to learn about the proper use of a serger, the aesthetic eloquence of dried flower arrangements, or the proper use of vitamins and herbs. (Things I don't give a damn about.)

My apartment has a prominent bookshelf and a few abstract paintings hanging on the wall. Being abstracts, the paintings can represent whatever I want them to for whoever is listening to my made-up explanations. Each one has had tens of stories made up about it, one of which might be close to the original artist's intent. But since each painting has tens of different artists whose names I don't even know if they exist, I feel confident that I am secure in my artistic flare. Along with the paintings, I have only pictures of my father and stepmother, and brothers and sisters. Family portraits are indicative of stability in relationships. I don't get along with my father, can't stand my stepmother, and think most of my siblings are weird. But neither they nor the woman I am trying to impress knows that. (I have the worn picture of my natural mother strategically placed in a Bible on the small lamp stand near my bed. When that sob story is needed, the proximity of the bed and its use in the intention plays into the scenario perfectly.)

"Who is Nietzsche?" my young waitress inquired.

"Can I fix you some pasta?" I responded with a smile from ear to ear.

Now back to not allowing a woman's personal belongings to be left in my apartment. After an intense session of sex that left that young waitress wanting more and willing to leave her boyfriend and move in with me, I got her dressed and drove her home. Since she was so distraught on the way to my apartment, she didn't know my exact address, and I didn't eat at the restaurant where she worked for a few months, so I wasn't worried about having to justify to her about our one nightstand.

Anyway, during the course of our intense release of "distraughtness." I had her take off one of her rings because it was in the way of my tongue when I licked her fingers. The ring got thrown aside in the heat of passion, and left behind when she left. The next morning, Marlee showed up with a steaming espresso and a morning paper. She knew I didn't have to work until later, and I parked my car in my assigned parking stall. As true as Murphy's Law seems at times, Casanova's Law never fails—Marlee found the ring and smelled the faint, lingering smell of another woman's perfume.

At that moment, my aunt became a foremost expert on the use of herbs and natural healing for food poisoning. I called her late last night because my symptoms had gotten worse. I didn't want to bother her, because I knew she had to get up early and work the next day. And it just so happened that the type of remedy she recommended involved a finger width portion of flaxseed. So she took off her ring, measured the portion to give to me, and forgot to put it back on.

The scenario came quick to my mind and relieved the tension that was building behind Marlee's brow.

That same day, I bought a bottle of flaxseed and keep it in my cupboard. You never know.

Satisfied that my apartment is in order, I lock it and walk the quarter mile to my strategically placed vehicle.

Tools of the Trade

I love sales. I've been a salesman most of my life—most of us are without even knowing it. When I was eight years old, I recall the tactics I used to sell my father the idea that it was necessary for me to spend the night at Garland's (my best friend back then) house when he already had said "No" three times.

The previous eight years had been spent figuring out what did and didn't work with my dad; so by the time I was eight, I was pretty good. I sold him on the fact that Garland's dad was working on a shed and they needed me to help. I waited breathlessly with this statement, hoping my dad (being pretty neighborly himself) wouldn't call up Garland's dad and offer his help. Luckily, my dad was busy himself and was probably sick of me asking, so he gave his permission.

That night was a glorious one for Garland and me as we rummaged through his mother's old issues of the Sears & Roebuck Catalog searching for the bra and panty section where our young bodies filled up with the preparatory pheromones that would eventually make us men. When his mother interrupted us with a plate of chocolate chip cookies and a couple glasses of milk, it was I who spoke first, "Garland, what page did you see that record player on?"

I was raised in a large family that consisted of seven brothers and four sisters, the youngest seven children coming from my father's second marriage. I was the third from the oldest and definitely the clown of the bunch.

For whatever reason he had, my father moved our family a lot. I went to 9 different schools in 7 different states from kindergarten through my senior year. For High School, I started 9th grade at one school, moved to another one in 10th grade, and spent half of 11th grade there. Then I was sent four states away to start the basketball season and await my family's eventual move.

My father decided not to move there after all, so he brought me back to my original 11th grade school. After just two weeks though, he decided he was moving to a different state than where he intended to move the previous month, so he sent me two states away to start the basketball season there instead.

Needless to say, I was always the new kid in town. Being the new kid in town requires a unique personality and a great amount of salesmanship if one intends on fitting in properly. Luckily, I was extremely gifted in athletics and made my way pretty easily with this talent. Getting to know the girls wasn't too hard for me either. By the time I was a Senior in High School, I had mastered the smile, the finesse, and the manipulation to win any girl's heart I wanted. In fact, I mentioned that half way through my 11th grade year I was sent two states away to a different High School. Well, two months into my tenure at this new school, I had become a hit with the office secretaries and vice principals. Anyway, one of the older, overweight secretaries, (I have always been drawn to this type), nominated me for Senior Class President.

After my nomination, one of the officers of the Pep Club took up the cause, and believe it or not, I won the election. Those who counted the ballots had to count them three times because I had only won by 2 votes. We didn't know what the hell a "chad" was back then, so the election was final.

No doubt, most of the girls voted for me, as well as the nerds, "druggies," and eventual dropouts. (I've always had a soft spot for the underdogs of society). The guy I beat in the election had lived in that area his whole life, grown up with all the kids that went to that school, and was dropped down to second string on the football squad when I showed up to play. (Ironically, we both played the same position in football.)

I wasn't well liked by most of the guys in the school, especially by that particular dude. I was accused countless times of trying to take away someone's girlfriend, but usually used my expertise in bullshit and manipulation to get myself out of many offers to fight. Oh yes, many males still have a primitive need to "lock horns" as the way to get the female. I didn't need to lock horns with anyone, nor did I need to strut my stuff. My "stuff" was who I really was—and the girls knew it, and the guys envied it.

My "stuff" evolved into my personality as I found myself alone, somewhat scared, needy, and longing for attention in the countless situations that my childhood circumstance had put me in.

If I wanted to, I could sell my birth certificate to my own mother, convince her that it was worth more than a government bond, confuse her as to who my real father was, and make her change the name of the man she listed as my father on the birth certificate to whatever man I wanted him to be. And she would still think I was her most honest son.

These personality traits aided me greatly as an Investment Broker, whose sole job is to sell other people's ideas, products, and services to potential investors. There wasn't a door I couldn't get into. There weren't too many dresses I couldn't get under either. However, in the professional world, a Player plays by different rules, yet the same tactics are used.

Ms. Caroline Channing is a perfect example. A client of mine had a great idea involving the use of the Internet as a virtual meeting place for single individuals who wanted to go on a cyber date instead of giving out his or her own private information. It was an ingenious idea, so I accepted the job.

Caroline Channing was the epitome of feminine success: beautiful, independent, very wealthy, and extremely intelligent. However, she was still a woman. I had never met her before, but knew she had money to invest. I called her office and asked to speak to her personally. Her secretary came back on the phone and asked who I was and what this matter was about. I briefly explained that I had an investment opportunity that Ms. Channing would be interested in. Channing's secretary was equally intelligent and very leery of a sexy voice on the telephone, so she defiantly insisted that I send some information through the mail and she would make sure Ms. Channing would see it. Yea, right! Channing probably received tens of "great" investment opportunities by mail every day.

Of course I didn't send anything in the mail. If I was going to get to talk to Carol Channing, I was going to have to appear in person and "play" her secretary first and then Ms. Channing. I dressed in my sexiest, yet still professional business suit, and wore a red tie. (Red does something for women.) I went to the bank, got a crisp new $100 bill, and headed for Ms. Channing's office. Luckily, security wasn't tight in the building, and I found her name inscribed on the office directory and headed up to the executive suites that she owned. (In fact she owned the whole building.) I went right to the head receptionist and asked which office was Carol's.

"Do you have an appointment?" the first receptionist asked, with that girlish smile that told me she liked what she saw.

I raised my index finger to my mouth and said, "Shhhhhh, I am a dear friend of hers and I want to surprise her." Her eyes pointed the way to Ms. Channing's secretary who had overheard the conversation.

"Is Carol busy with someone right now?" I asked Channing's personal secretary. Professional tact was required in this situation, so as not to upset the possibility of a good first impression. The secretary indicated that she would check her schedule, but before she could pick up the phone, my finger was to my mouth again and I was going through the office door of Ms. Caroline Channing.

She was a little startled to see a strange man enter her office without being forewarned by her now puzzled secretary, but a sincere smile and a glance from my "you're the sexiest woman in the world" eyes, gave me a brief moment to reach in my pocket and pull out that crisp $100 bill.

"Forgive the interruption Ms. Channing, may I call you Caroline? Man, you are much more beautiful in person than what one reads in the press." With that I introduced myself and handed her my card and the $100 bill. I told her that if what I was about to introduce to her was not an investment she wanted to make, she could keep the $100 bill for her time, and I would graciously leave. Ms. Channing sat back in her chair and listened to my explanation of the particular Internet dating service that I was pitching. Instead of making up a hypothetical situation demonstrating the potential of the dating service by using made-up people, I used her and me as the couple who met on the Internet. I explained exactly how I would use this new idea to take her on a cyber date.

By the time I was done with my hypothetical situation, I had no doubt that Ms. Channing was wet. Her eyes could not hide the fact. However, in a professional setting, she wasn't about to say anything that would disclose the fact that she wanted me. She politely asked if I would leave the literature and prospectus with her and she would review it. I agreed to leave the literature and asked if I could call on her in a couple of days to see what she thought about the idea. Normally, I would have gotten my $100 back at that time, because there was no indication that she did not want to make an investment; but I knew from the look on her face, the way she talked to me, and her handshake, that I would be getting more than $100 out of this deal.

Carol Channing did not invest anything into the company that I had introduced to her at first, but we must have had sex 20 times before I broke her professional pride by explaining that it was probably not very professional of me to take advantage of a potential investor in this way. Of course she said she didn't mind, and was even quite upset that I didn't want to have sex with her any more. But I was tired of her, and I already had gotten my $100 back in 4 shirts, 2 pairs of shoes, a suit, very expensive wines and dinners, and access to her mansion anytime I had the desire.

After her phone calls were not returned on numerous occasions, I then received a check for commissions on the sale of a substantial amount of stock purchased by none other than Ms. Caroline Channing. I received one more call pleading for me to see her after her investment was made, but I didn't return it. I was a player; I was a salesman—I sold and played her.

Women aren't the only ones that I sell my wares to. True, they are the only ones that I get something from besides money, but men are just as gullible to the right techniques, especially gay men.

I find gay men the easiest to sell to. They learn to develop a trust for me very quickly. Their hardening cocks don't hurt the outcome of the techniques that I use on them. I have never been with another man, and probably never will, but my gay clients don't know that. I pitch them like I do a woman, but use the professional rules of conduct to control any of their intentions meant for outside the realm of the deal we were working on. Straight men are another story. I hate straight men, especially professional ones.

Professional men do not like to be looked down to, argued with, or feel controlled in any way. They want to believe that their cock is the biggest at the meeting and no other can compete. Men measure cocks in different ways. Not just by the size, but by the presence of the one carrying it around.

The Japanese have a custom of bowing their head upon meeting. If a man is of a lower status he must bow his head lower than the man who has the higher status. I figured out this male ritual as soon as I witnessed it for the first time in a business deal I was pitching to some Japanese executives. The lower you bow your head the further down you have to reach to suck your own dick. The high-class Japanese barely bow their head in a show that they don't have to bend down much to reach their big dicks. Knowing this, every time I meet a Japanese businessman, I throw my head back with a gesture of "How ya doing, Partner?" They think this is American Southern hospitality. No, it's saying, I have to throw my head back to reach the top of my humongous cock.

Just kidding about the head thing, but I still hate professional, straight men.

The fact is, I act almost gay-like when I am pitching my wares to professional men. I come across confidant in my products, intelligent and knowledgeable in what I am doing, but with an air of "You can kick my ass anytime you want, your Big Dickness." God, I hate men, but I can sell them anything as long as I act like a woman.

Fishing

My career isn't the only professional expertise I have mastered. I have hobbies too. I love to fish.

The great outdoors has always appealed to men. Getting back to nature seems to be a male ritual of sorts. And fishing is the choice of many. (I thought hunting was the choice of the majority—hence the change.) There is something about fishing that makes a man feel like he hasn't lost his connection with nature.

Men imagine that each fishing trip will end with the catch of a better fish than the time before. There's a male intuition involved in being successful at fishing. First, you have to know what kind of fish you want. There are some fish that are very abundant and easy to catch. But the good ones…well, they take some planning and some knowledge and finesse to land. A man has to know where to fish, what kind of bait or lure to use, how deep he needs to sink it, how fast or slow to move it, and how to reel it in without losing it. With his knowledge and experience, mundane fishing becomes an adventure.

Usually you can't see the fish you want to catch. You know they are there because they have been caught before. Sure, you can throw a deep sinking piece of stinking meat to the bottom of any body of water and pull up the garbage fish that linger there—inactive, overweight, and virtually comatose. But to pull in the trophies, you've got to have skill.

A Pro prepares his rod and reel just right. He inspects each piece to assure that its function is doing what it is supposed to do and is ready for the "big one." He carefully chooses which bait he is going to use. He reads some books, watches some fishing shows, listens to advertisers, and gets advice from friends. Ultimately though, his choice of bait comes down to what he personally feels will get the bite—male's intuition. He threads the line, choosing the appropriate one, not too big, not too little—but just right to entice the fish to bite, and be able to reel her in. He baits the hook carefully, knowing that he might only have one chance, and when the fish nibbles, he wants to make sure setting the hook is successful. As he finishes baiting the hook, his anticipation grows. His heart beats a little faster—he can't wait to get the hook in the water.

The cast is his alone, personally developed from years of experience. Gently he raises the rod above his head, over his shoulder and behind him. Then with a sudden jerk, he releases the line so that it flows like silk across the top of the water. The bait lands softly in the water and sinks to the predestined level determined by the leader line meticulously chosen upon preparation.

Then the fishing really begins.

He holds his pole gently, but with control. He takes a few turns of the reel to assure that everything is ready. Then with the finesse of a puppeteer, he begins to make that bait dance in front of its hopeful recipient. He waits patiently, yearning and anticipating the first strike that tells him it is time to set the hook.

The fish are there. There are all kinds: fat ones, skinny ones, ugly ones, beautiful ones, ones that taste good, and ones that don't; but there are plenty. They see the bait, they smell the bait, and sometimes they will swim close enough to get a little feel about it. But the fisherman has baited the hook with a specialized attraction that only a few of the fish are interested in. These few interested fish swim closer and closer, eyeing the bait trying to figure out if they are hungry or not. Some might not be, but believe that this last enticing morsel might be all they will find for awhile, so they remain interested.

Now, fish aren't as stupid as they seem. A fish that has been hooked a few times is a little bit leery about anything that looks too good to be true. If there existed a fish philosopher, I am sure he would say, "If it looks too good to be true, then it probably isn't." But who listens to philosophers anyway?

Up above, the fisherman continues his choreography and senses that there are fish examining his well-timed moves. He waits; he dances; he's ready.

The experienced fish are swimming closer to the bait trying to give themselves any reason they can for not taking it. But before they know it, a beautiful member of their species happens upon the scene. This fish is big and beautiful, but inexperienced with the tactics of the predator that lurks above in the light. She sees the bait, has no reservation, and takes it all—hook, line, and sinker.

With one mighty yank, the fisherman sets that hook so securely that she doesn't even know what hit her. Frantic she tries to escape, but the hook is deep and secure, the line is strong, and the fisherman is playing the fight just right. She doesn't have the strength to fight this master of the light, and eventually gives up as she is pulled into the light, out of her environment and into the realm of the one who now controls her destiny.

You might ask why I speak about fishing. Well, I am a professional fisherman too. I fish for women. You could follow the above scenario allegorically to understand how I get close to nature—my ritual, my passion, my expertise.

Of course I love to fish. I am a man.

Daddy's Little Girl

To make a woman fall in love, it is essential that a Player understands why a woman falls in love, how a woman falls in love, and when is she the most vulnerable to make the fall. To understand these things, a man has to understand something that not even a woman herself understands—he has to understand how a woman thinks.

To accomplish this monumental task, one has to trace the development of a woman from her birth to adulthood. Psychologically speaking, all the events that occurred after a woman's 5th birthday can be discounted and ignored when it comes to understanding what makes a woman fall in love. From her 5th birthday on, the inquisitor will find all the events and experiences that a little girl goes through that will cause her, as a woman, to fall out of love with a man.

The first few years of any individual's life are defined as the "learning years," the years that lay the foundation for the rest of that person's existence.

A woman's first experience with falling in love comes along about the age of two, when she falls for the man who helped give her life. She falls in love with her father. This man takes care of her, spoils her, kisses her tenderly, and caters to her every need. In his arms the fetal woman feels safe, secure, and full of trust. She loves no one as much as she loves her father as she is wrapped in a warm, fuzzy blanket of codependency—there's that word again that means "being in love." During these early years, a woman learns how, when, and why to fall in love.

This filial honeymoon can last to about 5 years of age. After this time, the little girl begins to realize that her "Knight in Shining Armor" likes sleeping with her mother more than with her, and that the squeals and moans coming from her mother behind the closed bedroom door are not caused by Daddy's whiskers. She begins to sense that her father enjoys a different kind of relationship with her mother than he does with her. Jealousy forms in her little brow, and she loses some faith in her relationship with daddy. Freud called it the Electra Complex and rationalized that the little girl was jealous that her daddy had a penis and she didn't—bullshit! The little girl became old enough to start realizing what her real status in Daddy's life was. She felt a little betrayed and thus started her quest to figure men out. Good luck!

After the first betrayal and realization of "Mommy gets to have sex with Daddy and I don't," the pre-woman begins to search for the feeling that she felt before her father's infidelity to her. She searches to be in love—codependency towards a man. Right after the betrayal is when the woman is most vulnerable to make the fall. She wants to quickly replace the hurt with something satisfying, something warm and fuzzy, something that replaces "Daddy." And why does a woman fall in love? Because she was taught what a man is supposed to be like, what he is supposed to do for her, and how he is supposed to make her feel when she was only 3 years old.

There was more than one reason for my desire to study psychology and philosophy in college, and obtaining a degree was not one of them. I am the ultimate father figure to the woman I set my sights on. I take care of her, spoil her, kiss her tenderly, and cater to her every need. In my arms the woman feels safe, secure, and full of trust. She loves no one as much as she loves me, and she is wrapped in a warm, fuzzy blanket of codependency—the fool falls in love with me. But this time she gets to hear the squeals and groans coming from her own lips as I introduce her to the only thing that makes me want her—yes, my codependency—the world of ecstasy.

Maybe Freud was on the right track when he introduced the Oedipus Complex wherein the son falls in love with his mother. Maybe that's when the little boy learns how to be in love with a woman. Oedipus was a mythological character who really didn't exist. Maybe my mother really didn't exist, and my longing for her was no more real than the love Oedipus had for his mother. I hate mythology.

I guess it's appropriate here to introduce one of my current "daughters"—hypothetically speaking, of course.

Her name is Marlee Monet. Semantically French, and physically voluptuous, Marlee Monet had codependency written all over her face when I first laid eyes on her. I was visiting a local museum where I had met a few of my former conquests, when Ms. Monet passed by me. A good Player has superb peripheral vision and can see a woman looking at him long before she catches herself checking him out. Marlee didn't hide the glance and lingered at it until my own glance met hers. My "you're the sexiest woman I have ever seen" look made her blush and turn away. A woman is funny that way. They want a man to notice her, but do not want to be too conspicuous that she wants to meet him. Men—we don't care how conspicuous we are. We whistle, stare, grab our crotches, ask for a number, and even invite the woman to fuck us right there when we want her. But a father should never act that way towards his daughter. And a good Player never acts that way towards a woman.

I knew she wanted to get to know me from the way she glanced at me, smiled, and quickly looked away. But my glance and subtle smile was the fisherman dancing with the line, making the bait move in just the right way to entice a nibble. I was looking for a certain type of fish. Marlee was certainly beautiful enough, but there was more line and hook manipulation to be done before I knew if this was the one I wanted to hook.

I found an abstract painting and continued to look at it inquisitively trying to appear as if I was really interested in the piece of shit painting that looked like a painter filled his bladder with different colors of paints and pissed all over the canvass. However, if anyone had asked, I would have raved at the personality that the piece exuded. The sharp lines and defined strokes of what was obviously a camelhair oil brush that was kept fairly moist by the artist to assure that the impressionistic ideal was met. "Can you feel what the artist is trying to tell us?" I would ask any who stood close by. "I feel he was attempting to emit a touch of Picasso with an influence of Bucher and a definite European theme. But in his attempt, he failed to capture the essence of these artistic masters, yet has shared with us a unique piece that can be ubiquitously seen as virtuous and original.

Hell, I don't know the difference between crayons and watercolors.

You have to be patient to hook the trophies. I waited about 20 minutes in the same spot while Marlee went through the countless anxieties that a woman goes through as she considers introducing herself to a stranger.

"He's probably married, or gay! Most men that look like that are either married or gay. God, I would just die if I went up and started to talk to him and his girlfriend or wife walked up! What if he's not interested? I'll be so embarrassed! He wouldn't want to meet me; I am probably not the kind of girl he dates. His eyes, God they're gorgeous! It won't hurt if I just walk by him one more time and see if he notices me. But what if he thinks I am interested in him? Will he think I am too forward? Will that turn him off? If he were interested in me then he would come up and talk to me! Yea, I'm worth having, and if he wants a chance at me, I am going to make him work for the chance! But, where is he? Where did he go? Did he not notice me looking at him? I know he did, he smiled back at me. That means that he might be interested in me. It's not going to hurt to just walk by him again and check out his butt."

Sure enough, I caught the image of Ms. Monet approaching my location from the trained peripheral vision that would make Superman jealous. I made sure my hands were folded neatly behind my waist, holding in any portion of my sweater that might have been covering the curvature of my ass. When she was about 10 paces away from me, I bent toward the painting (which I had been staring at in disgust for the last twenty minutes), and slightly pushed out my butt for her to inspect. I paid no attention to her. I was making her sweat. I didn't want it to appear like I just wanted to have sex with her, now did I? As she passed in back of me, I cocked my head towards the bottom part of that pissed on piece of art as if inspecting one of its finer points, and was able to twist my head unnoticeably backwards to catch her checking out my ass.

I let her pass on by without giving the slightest hint that I noticed her. When she was about 10 paces away from my right side, I took my turn to check out her ass. Wow! What an ass! An onion ass. An onion ass is a term a Player has for the nicest asses out there. They are so nice they make you cry!

She disappeared out of my sight, but if my fisherman's intuition was not mistaken, she had stopped just out of sight to appear as if she was interested in another of the disgusting pukes that hung on the museum wall. There, she would be going through more anxiety trying to figure out if she should go back and introduce herself. Most trophies don't go back and introduce themselves. They know that if the fisherman wants them, he will use his bait to attempt the hook. Those fish who would bite at anything are not the desire of the Pros.

I walked in the direction that she had walked, turned a rounded wall, and found her admiring a painting. As soon as I appeared in her not-so-trained peripheral vision, she stood on her tiptoes, stretching her neck to take notice of some interesting part of that painting. As I got nearer and nearer, her heart began to beat faster and faster, wondering if I was just going to walk by or come up and talk to her. Women love confident men who are not too pretentious, but are unafraid to approach them.

I walked up right next to her and begin to flip that leader line around like a ballerina's final audition to be picked to perform on Broadway.

"So, what do you think about this piece?" I asked her with confidence.

This brazen approach caught her off guard, and it became very apparent that she was not experienced at meeting strange men in public places. She did and said all the wrong things if she was trying to keep me from realizing that she wanted to meet me.

"Oh, hi! I noticed that you take quite a bit of interest in some of these works yourself," she said, trying to hide the fact that her heart was racing and her facial pores were filling up with blood.

"Actually, I hate them." I kindly responded. A good Player knows that he must maintain control of the conversation if he wants to control the situation. Throwing out a statement that is totally unexpected usually does the trick. Women also have a tendency to make immediate judgments of a man from the first thing that comes out of his mouth. Marlee actually thinks I tell the truth.

"Oh," she said surprisingly.

"I came into the museum today because I was a bit bored. I walked around, caught your eye, and waited to see if you would come back around so I could meet you," I said with a carefully placed look into her eyes and a sincere smile. Now she knows I tell the truth.

"So, what makes you think I wanted to meet you?" she smiled back.

"I didn't know if you did or not, but thought that I wouldn't get much sleep if I let the opportunity of meeting you pass. From the first time your eyes met mine, my mind could think of nothing else but what might be lurking behind those beautiful brown eyes. And now upon meeting you, I can sense that there is much more to this beautiful woman than what she is letting me see. And with that, let me introduce myself…"

Ms. Monet had one of the best sets of tits that I have ever had the pleasure of enjoying. They were definitely one of her best physical assets, even more so than her butt, but I know one thing: never, never get caught looking at those gorgeous mountains of lust and joy while attempting to set the hook. So as to avoid even the temptation, I didn't take my eyes off of hers.

"Well, I am very flattered," she responded, quite impressed by my perceived honesty and boldness. "I did notice you, and thought it would be nice to meet you too."

"Really!" I sounded surprised that she would have a desire to meet innocent ol' me. "In that case, I stand preeminently more flattered than you, and for just cause—you are absolutely stunning."

I set the hook.

We spent the next hour talking about her past and my lies. Marlee was 26 years old and had never been married. She had various boyfriends growing up, but astonishingly was still a virgin. Normally, I would have ended the relationship right then and there. I don't have time to teach a woman how to fuck and cum. I wanted someone that was experienced and ready to cum as soon as I entered her. Virgins bleed.

But I wasn't about to pass up the chance of feeling that ass and handling those absolutely awesome tits. And the fact was, I hadn't introduced a virgin into the world of multiple orgasms for many years. They do have very tight pussies and are usually totally unaware of the games men play.

When she asked me about some of my former relationships, I told her how the last woman that I loved cheated on me and broke my heart, and that since that time, I hadn't dated much. I told her I had recently decided that it was much nicer to at least have a friend to do things with than be alone.

"Do you like pasta?" I finally asked her. "I make a great pasta dish!"

Being a virgin, Marlee had her own set of strict rules, and one of them was to never go over to a man's house until she got to know him better. She still lived at home with her parents, and I could tell she loved her father—can you see me smiling?

I mentioned that I wasn't doing anything that evening and if she would like, maybe we could meet somewhere for coffee and dessert, thus maintaining the façade that I really respected her for not wanting to jump right into the sack with me. However, that male intuition—the one that fishermen have—convinced me that I would have my hands all over those luscious breasts by the time the night had ended. By the third date, I would be the first to cup his hands around that tight ass and introduce Ms. Monet into a realm that she had no idea existed.

We mauled over ideas of where to meet, until I suggested that we invite her parents to come with us, because I knew a great place where I had recently taken my parents and they had had a wonderful time.

What a sweet gesture. I knew damn well that she didn't want her dad and mom tagging along on a date with her, but with that one suggestion, she put down her guard, gave me her home telephone number and address, and told me she would be ready by 7 PM.

When she was a little girl her daddy made her feel warm, safe, and secure. The thought being introduced into her mind of having her father along with us on our first date was all that was needed for her to acquiesce to my intentions. I used the same tactics that work for hypnotists and advertisers that use subliminal messages to change the thought processes of their audience. She was being carefully reeled into the light. That fish was now inside my boat—my world, in which I was the master of her fate.

I gave her a gentle but firm hug as we parted ways at the museum. I thanked her for the opportunity she gave me in meeting her, and almost made her faint when I took her two hands in mine and told her that I was looking forward with anticipation for the events of that evening. In her mind, it meant some great conversation with a hot cup of espresso warming her hands. In my mind, it was her warm breasts warming mine.

Playing the Game

I rushed home with a hard dick and began preparations for the seduction. I had no doubt that I could convince her to come back to my apartment that night, so I made sure it was picked up and all things were in order. I even checked the Bible on the nightstand to assure that good ol' mom's faded picture was still there. It was.

For a moment, I looked at my mother and wondered what it was like when my father took away her virginity. Was he gentle? Was he kind? Or was he just an asshole who wanted to fuck her? I wondered if it was a special moment for her when I was conceived. I hoped that when my father made love to her that night over 35 years ago, that he did so with respect and love for her.

My mind drifted off for a moment, and I saw my father gently holding her after he had introduced into her body the final ingredient that was needed to create me. He loved her, caressed her, and told her what a wonderful woman she was. He played gently with her hair as she lay next to him, their naked bodies entwined in the joy of peace and satisfaction that happen immediately after the act of making love and climax. I saw my mother smile as she looked into the eyes that he had just passed on to me in that one small cell. I loved my parents right then and longed to see them together.

But you fucked another woman, Dad! You bastard! You broke my mother's heart and drove her out of your life. Yet, you didn't stop for a moment did you, Asshole, to consider that your life consisted of four little boys and a little girl who needed their mother. You didn't think for a fucking moment what your throbbing dick was doing when you stuck it into that whore that you decided to fuck instead of my mother! You fucker! You broke my mother's heart and she broke mine! I hate you, Dad. You're nothing but a fucking man!

My face was wet with tears as the thoughts of my parents' breakup slowly dwindled away to where they belong—deep inside my heart where all my pain is stored. A place that is covered with my longing to fuck women like my father fucked the woman that caused my mother's heart to break. I didn't want to make love to a woman; I wanted to fuck her. I didn't want to marry a woman and take the chance of breaking her heart like my father broke my mothers. I was a Player. Players fuck to be needed, and become dependent upon needing to be fucked. I, too, am a fucking man like my father.

I put the photo back and picked up the telephone. It was Wednesday night, time for me to call the other two women in my life and let them know I was thinking about them.

"Hey Baby?" I happily exuded over the phone after Amy had answered. "How's the queen of my thoughts?" With that, I listened to Amy relate the events of her day while I thought about how I was going to seduce Marlee tonight. "Yea, uh huh," I responded at the appropriate times. I let Amy know how much I missed her and how much I wanted to see her tomorrow, the day that we usually met at her place for dinner and a great night of sex. Thursday evening her ex-husband had her two boys for the evening and took them to school Friday morning. It was the perfect opportunity for us to spend some intimate time together.

When it came to sex, Amy was one of the most enjoyable that I have experienced. Men get a kick out of watching a woman cum. The more times a man can make a woman cum, the studlier he feels. I am far from insecure with my ability to please a woman, but after a night of sex with Amy, I felt like I had a magic wand instead of dick, which with each magical thrust turned Amy's vagina into a gushing sea of cum. I have never seen anyone cum so much in my life. She must have had at least 8 to 10 orgasms with each episode. One night I actually timed her with the digital alarm clock that she had on top of her television in her bedroom. After some foreplay that lasted about 10 minutes, she climbed on top of me and fucked me non-stop, for 48 minutes straight. I couldn't believe it—orgasm after orgasm. I was totally soaked with cum from my upper chest to my knees. And when Amy cums, she really cums! She's one of the lucky few who ejaculates cum much like a man, except hers is very moist, warm, and plentiful.

How I held on and stayed erect is a mystery to me. It could be that I was so in awe about her ability to have so many orgasms that sex with her became surreal and I felt like I was an observer instead of a participant. It wasn't the best sex I have ever had, but it certainly was enjoyable to watch all the action.

I met Amy about 4 months ago at a Do-It-Yourself carwash. She was there washing her car with her two boys, ages 4 and 6. One of them got out of the car when Amy wasn't watching and ran. He was headed for a busy street when his mother caught sight of him. I was already getting out of my car to head the little guy off in case his mother didn't notice him.

Anyway, Amy screamed and threw the spray gun down to chase her son. The boy thought it was a game to get Mom so excited, so he kept running from her. While they were running away, I got a great glimpse of Amy's ass and her tan legs, exquisite examples of pure femininity. She definitely had one of the nicest asses I had ever laid eyes on. It wasn't just an onion ass; it was indescribable.

That little boy gave me the chance that all Players look for. While his mother was chasing the 6 year old, the 4 year old got out of the car, and after not finding his mother anywhere in sight, begin to cry. He went around the car and found himself face to face with the spray gun that was still squirting out water. The gun was winning the war, and that little boy just stood there crying, drenched by the gun's spray. I ran over, picked up the wet little thing, took control of the spray gun, and waited for his mother to return.

Amy showed up red-faced with the ear of a wincing 6-year-old in her hand. That's when her eyes first met mine. There I was, wearing a pair of Levi cutoffs, tanned legs, and a tank top shirt that exposed the hair on my chest, which was now quite wet because of the her youngest son's drenching experience. That wetness exposed the outline of my sculptured chest, and for a moment, Amy paused in a stare. When she finally regained control of her senses, she put the 6-year-old back in the car and approached me to take the younger one.

She graciously smiled and thanked me. I didn't notice a wedding ring, so I baited the hook.

"Why don't you go ahead and sit inside of your car with your two boys and I'll gladly finish washing your car for you," I offered with that look in my eyes that told her I really cared.

Women love men that care. Players have a saying: "The more they think that you care, the more they are sure to bare!"

Primarily, a woman wants a man to care for her above all else. However, if a man wants to make a surefire impression that will guarantee the service of that beating heart on a silver platter, a man has got to pretend to care about others.

Of course, the appearance and façade of caring is "real" caring to a player. Women don't have any idea about a man except for what comes out of his mouth. It's vital to the integrity and effectiveness of a compassionate mask that men watch what they say in front of a potential sex partner. That's why players are so charismatic and charming. I do not fake it when I present my caring, charming side to a woman. That is really who I am—there's no faking about it. And I am a very caring person to other's needs and also the needs of a woman.

What a Player does not care about, is what the woman is going to feel like when she finds out she's been hooked, hypnotized by the master of the light, jostled around a bit, and then thrown back in with the rest of the fish without a second thought from the fisherman. But does the Player remain caring and compassionate, charismatic and charming? You bet he does.

That's really what bothers me most about women. You have a relationship, and for whatever reason you chose not to continue it. In a Player's case, it's usually because they are bored with the sex and the capture-and-conquer thrill is over. So the guy never calls again, doesn't write, vanishes into the same world from which he appeared. Why should that bother a woman? He didn't ask her to marry him or give her any type of time commitment, he just frees the woman to go on with the same life that she had 4 to 6 months before he dumped her. But women don't like freedom. They don't like Players. They want to belong to someone, count on someone, love someone—Oh, I mean be codependent on someone.

Why can't women realize that a "one night stand" means: You are too fat or ugly for me, or you suck in bed, or you're not worth attempting to start a relationship with? Further, if they believe they have started a relationship and they haven't fucked the man yet—let's say they have in their little rule book that they won't let the man touch them until the third date—then they are aghast when after the act of "making love," which is what the woman wants the man to be doing to her instead of just "fucking" her, the guy never calls again. A man will allow the "rules" of engagement that a beautiful woman sets if she has the tits, ass, lips, or sexual appeal that entices him. However, if she sucks in the sack, he won't waste any more time on the relationship than the time it takes to "take her for a ride." He'll then get off the bike that doesn't feel good, and look for another means of transportation.

Get a grip, women! If we liked you and you are as hot as you think you are, then we'll come back for more. If a woman really wants to find out how "hot" she really is, or how good she is in the sack, find a Player, fuck him, and see if he calls you in the morning. If he doesn't, sit down, have a good cry—which should only last for 10 minutes at most—and get on with your codependent life. But don't blame it on the next guy you meet, or perhaps, you are going to scare off one of the few guys that really give a damn about anything other than sex. Nice guys hate "men haters."

After your cry, get off your overweight butt, eat right, exercise, and try to become the type of woman that you want to attract in a man. I'll walk into a bar to dance for some relaxation and possibly a one-night fling, and these overweight women droll, hoping for their chance to dance with me, fantasizing what it would feel like to have my toned body laying between their humongous thighs. To them it's a fantasy; to me it's sickening.

"Oh, all men are looking for is a woman with the perfect body," women complain as they get little attention from the men who have what they don't.

Well, duh!

Why don't you overweight women start dating the guys who look like you, and quit trying to fantasize that you are going to meet the perfect man, in the perfect body that is looking for more in a woman than just her body? There are many "nice guys" hidden behind the layers of fat and excess weight just waiting to get fucked by a woman their own size. Oh yea, all those women are looking for is a man with the perfect body. Pleeeeeeeease!

Now back to compassion.

A Player would never reveal the fact that he thinks the way I have just demonstrated in words in the above paragraphs. In fact, he shows a high amount of respect to overweight women and great compassion to the ugly ones. Does he do this because he likes what he sees? No. He does it because these women might have a girlfriend that is beautiful and looking for a compassionate, nice man who just so happens to be good-looking. Also, he is playing the fishing line a little, making it dance with finesse and beauty, because he never knows if a trophy fish is watching the action. Women love compassionate men.

It didn't take Amy long to believe that I really cared about her and her two boys. I made it a point to miss her car with the nozzle and soak the front of my shirt and shorts revealing the cut line of my pectorals and the wet protruding fly area of my pants where her mind was left to imagine the contents it might contain. With each swipe of the foaming brush, I made sure my flexed triceps were hard and defined. Every once in awhile, I would find one of the boys putting his face up to the window to get a better view of the strange man that was washing their car. A quick smile and a squirt from the nozzle sent them giggling to their seat and left a "God, I want this guy" smile spread all over their mother's face.

I spent longer than usual washing her car that day, but Amy didn't mind, and neither did I. I rinsed off the car and waved for her to pull her car forward so that I could pull mine in. I knew that if she were truly as wet inside as I was outside, then she would not drive off before she got out of her car to thank me. She pulled up to the vacuums stationed near the carwash and I pulled into the same stall where I had performed my dance. Sure enough as my instinct is alive and well, she got out of her car and headed toward me. That's when I really got a good look at the way her legs and butt contoured into her upper body. Not much for tits, but oh what a nice ass! She threw a tuft of her blonde hair to the side and smiled at me, never taking her eyes off mine.

"That was sure nice of you to help me with my boys and wash my car," she said a little shyly, totally turning me on.

I had already put my money in the slot and was holding an already blasting spray nozzle when she stopped just outside the wash bay.

"No problem at all. I love kids!" I promised.

"Can I pay you for washing my car for me? I know you put a couple of your own quarters in to finish the rinse cycle," she offered. She stood there talking even though I was starting to spray down my car with the wash water. That's when I knew she was mine for the taking.

About that time, both of the boys were headed out the car door chasing each other around the vacuum area. I motioned toward them as I told her that I needed no pay to be of service to a mother that looks like she could use a hand from time to time. She turned and ran to corral the two cowboys. Oh what an ass I was observing running to lasso her kids. I was going to get me a piece of that ass very, very soon.

She caught her kids and herded them back into the car and seat-belted them in, bending over each time she reached in to buckle them up giving me a couple more shots of the ass that she, at this time, didn't know I was even interested in. With her boys secure, she turned once more toward me, waved, and thanked me. That's when I set the hook.

"Do you and your boys like spaghetti?" I yelled out.

Not really knowing if she had heard me correctly, she glanced briefly inside her car, told the boys to stay put, and walked back over to the wash bay where I was even wetter and my muscles more defined. I got her name, number and address, and set a time to meet her that evening at her place to cook spaghetti.

Now some might say that Amy was crazy for giving a stranger her phone number and address so soon. But was I a stranger to her? What stranger would hold her son while she chased down the other, wash her car without needing to be asked, and not pay any noticeable attention to an ass that is probably used to being gawked at by every man that passes her by? And who shows interest in the safety of her kids before showing interest in her?

Yes, I was strange all right. Strange to her inner sense that told her that this man was different than the others. This man is compassionate, caring and considerate of others, and to top it all off, gorgeous. This man couldn't be a Player who is only interested in sex, now could he? She'll never know until she has to sit down for 10 minutes and get over me.

On the phone I assured Amy that I would miss her tonight and asked to say hello to her two boys. I have a soft spot for children—most Players do. I grow attached to the children of my women and usually end up missing them more than their mothers. Maybe I see in their curious eyes and natures what I hoped that others saw in me when I was a child. I hoped that they would not turn out like me—desperately needing, hopelessly yearning for new adventure and thrills. Hopefully they will love their mother and have one to love them throughout their crucial younger years.

I love watching children as they play, as they deal with life like only a child can see it. I often try to see through their eyes and understand adults the way they understand them. I want to be one of them again, and I do not want them to become me.

If You Got It, Flaunt It

I say hello to Amy's boys, tell their mother that I am horny just to hear her voice, and hang up so I can prepare my small, comfortable apartment for my new conquest, Marlee.

I knew I would possibly be meeting her parents tonight when I picked her up, so it would be important that I dressed conservatively. Yet I knew that some sex appeal had to exist to tickle Marlee's interest. The right kind of foreplay that leads to sex starts when the man is getting dressed.

Clothes designers spend lots of time and money trying to figure out what people want to wear. And they are well aware that the consumer wears different outfits for different purposes. Sex sells. The fashion industry knows it, the advertising industry knows it, the business world exploits it, and Players take advantage of it. The right kind of clothes can make the difference between sex appeal and an ordinary person. A person has got to flaunt his or her best parts so that the enhancement becomes an enticement. Makeup is out of the question if a man wants a woman to think he's a man. So a "real" man is stuck with whatever he can wash off, pluck out, or shave off his face. However the clothes are different; they can make the man.

I choose a conservative sweater that is one-half size too small for me with patterns running horizontal along the chest area. The horizontal lines cast a slight visual illusion that the chest is larger than it really is. The ½ size increment allows the sweater to fit the pectorals perfectly, emanating a natural look of strength and stability. Three buttons run up the neck area of the sweater. Two will be open, the third closed—just enough exposure to show some chest hair, but not enough to make it appear like I want anyone to notice.

The right pants are harder to find. Each manufacturer has its own style and form. When a man finds just the right one, he will stick with the brand. (Very good way to tell if a man wears his pants to impress or just to cover his sloppy butt and small dick. Check and see how many different brands of pants he wears.) If he sticks to one brand, you know he cares a lot about how it presents his wares. I choose one that fits tighter on the waist and buttocks, but not so tight in the thigh region. My particular brand has a way of making my ass and penis area stick out farther than they really do.

The ass and penis areas are like magnets to the cold steel eyes of a woman who uses stealth technology to conceal the fact that her eyes are attracted to these male erogenous zones. Heaven help the ego of a woman if she is discovered looking at a man's ass or penis area. Women don't do that! Bullshit! If it were proper for a woman—and it usually becomes proper when she gets a few drinks in her system—she would be checking out every guy's ass that passed her by, and fantasizing of it thrusting itself methodically and forcefully between her legs. And the penis—women just plain love penises. And they don't fool anyone but themselves when they say size doesn't matter. Size does matter. And if a man can find a pair of pants that exaggerates his size, he'll stick with them like crazy glue.

To wear a sweater and pants like the ones I wear, when one meets the parents, would be suicidal to a first impression. Parents, believe it or not, are human too. If the mom sees a nice looking man with a gorgeous chest, bulging lower portions and great eyes, she's going to get wet. To cover up her lust for her daughter's date, she is sincere and sweet through the introduction, but as soon as her daughter leaves with him, she is bitching to her husband how she doesn't trust that man with her daughter—that she is concerned that her daughter hasn't made the right choice.

"Why can't she date Johnny next door? He is more down to earth and is a good boy." she'll comment, in hopes that her husband will agree. All this so that there is absolutely no indication given to her husband that she wants to fuck her daughter's date.

Now Daddy is different. He knows fully well that the guy wants to fuck his daughter at the soonest opportunity. He'd like to lock a chastity belt so tight around his daughter's breasts and vagina that even Houdini himself would turn to masturbation in frustration.

He also gets through the introductions with a smile and the ultimate fatherly question that gives old Dad's real intentions away, "So, what are you guys going to do this evening?"

I have always wanted to give an honest answer to this question.

"Well, first I am going to wine and dine your daughter, then try to get into her pants after she feels she must repay me for the evening, and if that fails, get her drunk and then fuck the shit out of her! Is that okay with you, Dad?"

Nevertheless, the Player usually ends up politely outlining an itinerary of joyous activities that will enlighten the evening of his daughter to such an extent that she will be anxious to relate the happy events in their entirety to her parents upon her return.

Of course, Dad is thinking, "Bullshit! He just wants to fuck my daughter." And why does he think this? Because he's a man.

Anyway, I pick out a jacket, that I purposefully call "the Cover," and lay it out ready to put on over my clothes to cover any protruding or explicit signs of "I am sexy and want to fuck your daughter." The jacket is one size too big, and its length smoothly covers my lower torso area. The jacket will be worn during the introduction and then taken off the first time we get out of my car.

The way it's taken off is just as important as why it is worn. It is worn to relieve pressure off the parents or the woman who might still be a little leery of a new man's intentions. When you get to the first place you are going, you park the car, get out with your jacket on, and go around and let your woman out of her door. Then you lock the car, take her hand, and begin walking towards where ever you are going. After about 10 steps, you stop, tell your date that you would probably be more comfortable without the jacket, and you turn around—her hand still in yours—and go back to the car. You let go of her hand and gently touch her shoulder about two steps before you get to the car. This tells her to stop and wait. But, inconspicuously you are telling her to observe.

You face her, remove the jacket by taking one arm out, and force out your chest as you remove the other. You give her a sincere "thanks for waiting for me smile," turn around, unlock your car door, and bend in to put your jacket inside, giving that woman the best view of your ass that you could possibly present. Trust me, by this time she saw your pecks, she sees your ass, and while you were bending over placing your jacket in the car, she opened her eyes wide, sighed softly to herself, and bit her teeth down.

You're dancing that bait right in front of her nose!

My clothes for the evening are laid out on my bed and then I chose the underwear. This first night with Marlee I don't expect to reveal my underwear or what they hold. She's a virgin, so things have to go a little more slowly than normal. My choice of underwear is random and I take little thought in what purpose they will serve tonight.

There on my bed is the outer covering of what I want to be tonight. It covers and aids in the process of getting what I want. I have dressed myself and picked out my own clothes as long as I can remember. I have no memories of a mother who picked out her son's clothes and lovingly dressed him for school.

My thoughts create an image of myself as a young first grader going to my first day of class at a new school. At an earlier time than usual my mother is at my bedside gently shaking my shoulder and whispering that I need to wake up and get ready for my exciting first day of school. She tenderly caresses my hair through her fingers as her eyes tear up, realizing that her little boy is growing up so fast. She helps me get dressed explaining how wonderful my first day of school is going to be. First she pulls over my head a small sweater that she knit with her own hands just for me—the lines are running vertical to make me appear taller than I really am. She carefully clasps the three buttons that are near the neckline, making sure that the top one is not so tight that it causes my small neck any discomfort. She tells me that she is proud of me and my desire to learn. She helps me put on my denim pants that fit just right for the little boy that she knows will wear holes in the knees by next week.

After presenting me in front of the mirror and telling me what a handsome boy I am, she picks me up in her arms and carries me into the kitchen. There, she has prepared a special "first day of school" breakfast of my favorite foods. I smell the fresh pancakes and homemade syrup that only she can make right. I taste the freshly squeezed orange juice and my tongue senses the little pieces of pulp that tickle as they go down my throat.

Everything seems so wonderful, so peaceful, so loving. After breakfast she helps me brush my teeth, and she puts the final touches on the hair that she hasn't stopped touching since she woke me up. She brings me my jacket and helps my tiny arms find their way into the right holes. She carefully zips it up until she reaches the neckline area where she makes a smooth transition of holding my zipper to holding my face gently as she kisses my forehead and again tells me how wonderful I am.

I leave the house with a smile, my backpack on my back, ready for anything. I turn back to get one more look at my mother who I know is smiling with a lump in her throat as she watches her little boy take his first step to becoming a man—but she is not there.

Victoria's Secret

"Fuck these goddamn clothes!" I scream with tears in my eyes. I pick them all up off the bed and throw them at the full-length mirror meant to assure me of their necessity.

The phone rings. I wipe the last remaining wetness from my face and regain the composure of a man.

"Hello," I always say with a confidence and gaiety that knocks the caller completely off guard. "Well Victoria, my gorgeous babe, I was just thinking about you, so I took a cold shower before I head to an appointment," I said with a player's charisma and swift thinking.

"Fuck!" I said to myself. "I forgot all about seeing Victoria tonight. Shit! What am I going to do?" This whole thought process of castigating myself for my lapse in memory, something I don't often do, and including the comment of my pending appointment, took about ½ of a microsecond. Thank God for a Player's brain.

Luckily for me, I hadn't confirmed any plans this evening to see Victoria, and I wasn't about to give up the chance to get my hands on the gorgeous breasts of a virgin, so it didn't take too much creativity to explain the necessity of my presence at a company meeting that would last late into the night. One of the corporate heads flew in for this meeting, and it was important that all employees be in attendance.

"Wait a second," I said to myself suddenly. I know that Marlee is a virgin and I probably won't be having sex this evening, and since she lives with her parents, they will probably expect her home at a reasonable time, so why give up the possibility of having some great sex tonight?

"You know, Babe," I continued with Victoria, "The meeting shouldn't last much past midnight. So go to bed early and be ready for my craving body to snuggle up against yours as soon as I am done."

This satisfied Victoria's female yearning to feel that she is important and needed. I ended the conversation contented in realizing that I was going to enjoy some fantastic firm breasts of a virgin French woman, and end the night with one of the most gorgeous pairs of lips I have ever known wrapped around an organ that deserves the succulent ambiance that Victoria's lips provide.

A Player's term for the best lips a woman can possess is "Kind Lips." They're called "kind lips" because they're the kind of lips you want to stick your dick in—and Victoria Bartel has the best. Men love full lips, but not too full. Some women have lips that are so full that they make it impossible for a man's lips and tongue to caress. Some of the best kissers I have experienced have been women with very thin lips. Women with thin lips seem to know how to use them better than women with more full lips. It's possible that a woman with full lips has the immediate attention and lust of a man, which causes the man to engulf the lips and overpower the kiss.

Women with thinner lips caress the man's lips more seductively in an apparent attempt to bring more attention to what seems to be a deficit in their sex appeal. This extra attention to the man's lips is noticed, and the man is quickly turned on. Before I met Victoria, I absolutely, positively, without reservation would have sworn to the fact that women with thinner lips kiss better than their fuller rivals. There has been only one time in my life that I almost came kissing a woman. She was a thinned lip woman who took my lips into her hers and manipulated them like no other woman ever has.

Men do not kiss like women. Men are forceful, lusting, wanting; ready to slam our dicks into those lips at whatever moment we're able. Women, on the other hand, know how to kiss. And the women that kiss the best, kiss how they want to kiss, and not how a man kisses. "Kind Lips" does not mean that the woman knows how to kiss.

A lot of women tend to kiss how men taught them. If a man wants to be a known as a good kisser, he will learn how to follow the lead of the woman. However, it's important that the man makes the first move towards the kiss, and then become the canvas.

Kissing is an art. It first starts with the artist's desire to create her masterpiece on a blank canvas using any colors that are available. The final composition is developed by the use of the brush. Any type of brush in the hands of a master will work to combine just the right amount of tints and tones to create the final piece. The strokes must be gentle at first, using just enough paint to give the background of the work the right mood.

When the background is ready, and the canvas becomes more pliable due to the moisture of the paint, then the artist can introduce deeper strokes—longer, more intense, and creative. The work begins to take form at this time, expressing the inner desires of the artist that only she understands. The brush becomes part of these subdued desires and releases the energy that is confined in the soul of the artist. When finished, the artist has expressed who she is and what she wants, and when she stands back to view her work, she is completely satisfied.

Now, gentlemen, how in the world can an artist do her work if the canvas is brittle, coarse, and is continually moving on the easel? Let the artist do her work, and she will create a masterpiece that both of you will long to admire over and over again. But whatever you do ladies, never, never verbally instruct a man on how to kiss. Not only will you blow his ego, but you will never be able to teach him how you want to kiss. He will feel anxiety instead of passion worrying about whether or not he is doing it right.

Let a man kiss you however he wants. If he doesn't meet your approval, then wait until he is done, tell him to close his eyes and relax his gorgeous face. (Make sure you use the word gorgeous.) With his eyes closed and his lips relaxed, he becomes the canvas. Now, gently paint the masterpiece that you desire. Eventually, you will control the kiss and the man. When a man is kissed just right, he is not just kissing. He is imagining what your lips and their motion would feel like on his penis—the "kind lip" syndrome.

Victoria Bartel has one of the best-kept secrets that every man dreams of—full lips and the artistic prose to use them.

The Dance Academy

I met Victoria at a dance. Not "dancing"—at a dance. A Player can go to any club that provides its constituents with alcohol, dancing, and lots of fish, and find someone with whom they can enjoy a "quickie" or a one-night stand. Most women go to clubs knowing full well that most of the guys they will encounter there want to have sex with them. A bar or club is an Elementary School for a Player. There he is taught the three "R's of the game: Recognize what you want, Remember to play it cool, and learn to Reel her in.

There are basically two reasons why women go to bars; they go to get attention, or they go to get fucked. Most do not go to find the "right" man. It's a commonly believed feminine dogma that "you'll never meet the right man in a bar." There are women, however, that need sex as bad as men do. These are the bottom feeders—those that can be caught by tying a stinking piece of meat to any size fishing line, throwing it in the pond with a huge sinker, and letting it sit on the bottom. There's no fisherman finesse in the attempt, only waiting. Sooner or later a desperate fish comes along who either hasn't eaten for a long time, or needs to eat to maintain its size. It grabs the piece of stinking meat that doesn't even have a hook in it, and hangs on until the fisherman pulls it up to the boat, fondles it, and then throws it back. You don't actually think its edible, do you?

The curriculum needed for the Elementary School of Players is the women that go to bars for attention. These are the majority of women that dress up sexy and hit the party scene in an effort to prove to themselves that they are still attractive and desirable. They have no intention of going home with a "man from a bar," and are usually satisfied with teasing men, making men want them, and having the experience when they turn men down. These women provide an Apprentice Player the opportunity to try out his skills, hone them, and eventually graduate to attend the University of Controlled Manliness, where he will pursue a Masters Degree in Feminine Conquest. Upon receiving this upper-class degree, a world of unlimited sex and companionship is guaranteed.

A graduated Player doesn't need to go back to Elementary School to learn what he already knows. So unless he wants just a quick sexual release, he avoids the bars and clubs. He goes places where women have their guard down. He finds places where women congregate with either an intention to "find Mr. Right" or a hope that the possibility exists.

Religious dances are a Player's smorgasbord. A woman attends these dances believing (with the same faith that adheres her to the religion) that God might aid in her search for a mate. Faith is the substance of things hoped for, the evidence of things not seen, right? (I hope I quoted that right. I don't even know where it's found.) Love is something that cannot be seen. The evidence of its existence is in the heart of the woman. This evidence becomes more tangible when a woman feels her heart flutter, her breathing increase, and her sweat glands open, as she is swimming around the bait and lures of an experienced fisherman. The substance of her hope is the sculptured chest, handsome face, gorgeous eyes, full hair, and sincere smile of the object of her faith.

A hypnotist, like a religious guru, knows that he or she cannot hypnotize anyone that does not want to be. When a Hypnotist is looking for members of an audience to aid in the presentation of the hypnotic act, he or she performs simple tests and asks certain questions in order to ascertain which members of the audience are susceptible to hypnosis. Only those with a predisposition to suggestion are chosen.

Most women who attend religious single's events are already predisposed to the idea that they want to meet someone. Their minds are open and ready, and their hearts are engulfed with the faith necessary to make anything happen. Usually they begin the evening with an intentional prayer or a silent one whispered in their head on the way to the dance. "Please, God! Let there be just one more nice man that thou hast reserved especially for me," they plead, with all the serenity of a daughter in distress, hoping that there's a loving father that will save her from her misery.

With their faith full and their heart open, they enter the dance and immediately check out every man there to see if "the Spirit" will bear witness that her beloved is in attendance. She scans each face, seeing many that she always sees at these singles' events. She carefully looks everywhere, inconspicuously of course, searching for him. Then she spots him. "Look at him standing there smiling. He's handsome, tall, and isn't walking around checking out every woman in the place. Who is he? Is he the one?"

Victoria Bartel stood across the dance room floor glancing at me whenever she could without seeming anxious to meet me. I noticed her the first time while she was dancing a slow dance with another man. I was dancing with my partner and noticed a pair of the "kindest" lips I had ever seen talking shyly with her dance partner. She threw her head back in a laugh responding to something her partner had said to her. As she brought her head back down near his shoulder, her eyes glanced my direction and caught mine. The glance was brief, but intense.

I kept my distance during the rest of the song, but swung my partner around enough times, at the right angle, to notice her looking at me whenever my head was turned and her partner was occupied feeling her breasts up against him. This time she didn't mind that the much older man she was dancing with held her close to him. When he did, she didn't have to look at him but could look where she wanted. Near the end of the dance, I made sure my dance steps took me near Victoria. Her partner spun her slowly around keeping her close, his dick obviously appreciative of her desire to keep her head from facing his. With that spin, her eyes met mine again.

This time I had threw the line out. I learned well in Elementary School. I recognized her, I remembered to play it cool, and I began to reel her in. Yet with my advanced degree, it came naturally—almost like a gift from God. I smiled one of the sexiest smiles I could muster.

I let Victoria dance with many other men that night and I made sure my partners and I danced in just the right way and in the right area to keep that lure bouncing—naturally dancing in front of her nose.

Finally, I went to the refreshment stand and got a cup of punch and a few cookies to occupy me while I watched Victoria on the dance floor. Two dances came and went. Victoria danced both of them and couldn't help but notice me checking her out. I kept sipping the punch and eating the cookies slowly to avoid having to dance with anyone who might ask me. My advance degree had taught me that it wouldn't take Victoria long to have the sudden urge to get a glass of punch and a cookie.

After she had danced the second time, knowing I was watching her, she politely excused herself from her partner and started toward the refreshment stand. Women that look like Victoria do not stand long at any dance. She was approached three different times by three different men during her 50-foot trip to the refreshment area. I watched as these desperate amateurs failed to win her attention. I felt sorry for the foolish bastards that were fishing way out of their league. Women hate this kind of man—hopeful romantics that pursue women way too good-looking for them. Players hate this kind of woman too.

I shifted slightly so that I could watch the action at the refreshment table. Sure as God created mankind, another man approached her and kindly served her a drink with a smile. "That was a cool move," I said to myself, impressed by the elementary schooling that this suitor obviously had. He didn't push Victoria to accept his offering, but kindly held out the option. Then I saw him make an elementary mistake that uncovered his lack of education. The idiot picked up a cookie with his own hand and offered it to her. Like she couldn't make her own choice of which cookie she wanted.

She kindly declined this offer and chose some celery instead. I saw her eyes roll up as she turned around. I turned so she couldn't see me watching, and giggled to myself about the poor bastard who just lost any chance that he might have had to impress her. I turned back toward her and was not surprised to find her standing right behind me. As I turned, she put her cup to those incredible lips, and her eyes glanced up and away from mine. I turned away again and smiled. "She's mine!" I assured myself.

She knew that I wanted to meet her, but because I didn't approach her, she figured I might be a little intimidated or too shy to approach someone I liked. "How cute," women often think when they encounter a good-looking man that doesn't seem to have the balls to approach them. "Maybe he's a nice guy," they convince themselves.

Not in this case. Not only did I have the balls that her lips would soon be sucking, but I also had the education and the background to understand that if I presented myself in such a manner, then I had already initiated a trust factor that is important to a woman. Furthermore, I was God's gift to her for her exceeding faith.

I finished my drink and cookies and headed to the nearest garbage can to deposit the empty cup and napkin. The route to the garbage can took me right by Victoria, who was enjoying her celery with an obvious anticipation that I would come up and talk to her. I didn't stop when my eyes met hers again. But this time I enhanced the smile with a gentle and deep "Hello," which resonated from the already toned vocal chords of one with a Masters Degree.

I walked back to the table searching without intent for another refreshment. My superbly developed peripheral vision allowed me to notice Victoria throw her cup away, look my way with a little frustration, and turn back toward the dance floor. She stood right on the edge of the floor waiting for the next song to begin. I decided to set the hook.

I walked up behind her just as she was being approached in front by another man. I hurried my stride just enough to grab her hand gently from behind as the other guy begin his proposal. Now, men are not the only ones with good peripheral vision. In fact, sometimes I wonder if women have eyes in the back of their heads. Victoria was well aware that it was I who was approaching her from behind. She gently squeezed my hand assuring me that she wasn't going to let me get away, as she kindly informed the man directly in front of her that she had promised this dance to me.

"It's about time you asked me to dance," she smiled. Her eyes met mine for the first time in a mutual stare. The stare only lasted a few seconds, but I know to her it seemed like an eternity. She buried her head in my shoulder and snuggled her body next to mine. I could feel that she had firm, real breasts and no excess weight. But not even her body warmth and desire could get my mind off of her absolutely perfect lips. I wanted another look at them.

"So, you really wanted to dance with me?" I asked innocently in her ear.

She pushed her upper body back from mine leaving her pelvic region stuck close to my groin. She smiled, and I sensed the pheromones inside my body rising to the visual ecstasy that her lips were illuminating. "You knew I wanted to dance with you," she sheepishly responded.

"Not really," I responded, trying to sound convincing. "I am not a member of your church and came to this dance to avoid the 'bar scene'."

I proceeded to convince her that I was not a religious man, but found that religious women appeal more to me than other women because of their morals and positive lifestyle. I mentioned that I had always wondered what her religion was like and what made people like her so happy. I knew I was opening up her heart and faith even more with my pretended interest.

Most religious people feel it an obligation to share their message with others. Since Victoria was now sure that God had his hand in our meeting, she also believed that God had sent me directly to her to satisfy her need of a man, and my need for a god. A Player calls it "Missionary Sex."

Victoria buried her head deeper into my shoulder and began to caress my arms with her warm hands. Her gentle unobtrusive pelvic thrusts told me that the Spirit was bearing down on her now. I pushed her gently back telling her that I wanted to peer in her eyes and see what it was that made her who she is.

By this time, it seemed to her that there was not anyone else on the dance floor but us. As we danced slowly, her eyes fixated on mine, I set that hook so deep it almost tore her lips off. After about 10 seconds of a romantic stare, I drew her gently closer. It was one of the moments where time seems to stand still—a movie moment where the characters are getting ready to kiss for the first time.

I gently parted her soft lips with mine and felt the moisture that was hidden behind them. I didn't use any tongue at this time, but allowed her to sense the desire that my mouth had hidden by lightly sucking her lower lip. Her upper lip was lying gently on top of mine where it fit—nestled perfectly. I pulled my lips away slowly allowing the moisture to linger in the warm air outside of our mouths. Her eyes were still closed when she softly sighed and dropped her head back to my chest. I was going to feel those lips around my dick tonight.

We ended up at her condo that evening with her anticipation showing me some of the writings of her religious leaders and discussing why she was so happy with life. I expressed my pretended interest in her faith, and during the early hours of the next morning, I was introduced to a missionary style of giving head that would make God himself cum.

Of God and Family

On the way home to my apartment the next morning I thought about the tactics I had used the night before to persuade Victoria that I was chosen by God for her. I remembered my father's persistence in making us attend Sunday School every week, fulfilling what he considered to be his obligation for my spiritual upbringing. When I approached my father to let him know I did not want to attend church, he rhetorically responded, "If you can tell me any better place where you should be on Sunday, then you can go there instead." Now, to a young child, anything was better than church. However, no matter how hard I tried to justify my necessity to visit the local swimming hole or go on a joy ride to town with my friends, Dad always seem to convince me, (as I felt slight pains of remembrance in my behind), that church was the best place to be.

Who was God anyway? Was he a man? If he was a man and made us in his image, then he gave us penises to use and desires to use them. Why then did he make me feel so terrible the first time I woke up and my underwear was moist from the ejaculatory release I had experienced during the night thinking about my sixth grade teacher, Miss Talkawski?

After this experience, I began to notice changes in my body and in my desires toward girls. I used to hate them. Now I wanted to see them naked. "This was bad. Very, very bad." I was taught to believe. I couldn't help it when my hand took hold of my hardened penis one day and begin to stroke it as my friends and I had imitated so many times at school. But when our local minister asked me if I touched myself in any unholy manner, I lied. I was petrified that I would lose my soul for masturbating. Hell, I didn't even know that "masturbation" was the proper term for "jacking off" until I read it as a young man of seventeen sitting on the toilet at my friend's house looking at the comics in his father's Playboy.

My father never sat me down and told me about the changes in my body. He was totally oblivious to the fact that the babysitter that he hired to watch me when I was younger would put me down for a nap right by her side. She would put my hand up her shirt and force my hand to caress her breasts. After a few times of playing with her boobs, she unbuttoned her pants and put my hand down between her legs where I got grossed out by the sticky moist hole my tiny hands found there. I thought this was what older girls wanted. "You're dad will think you are a bad, bad, boy if you tell him what you did to me!" the sitter would convince me.

God knew. If he knew, then why didn't e stop it? Why did he let a young boy be introduced to sex in this way, if sex was a bad thing? Where was he when that little boy was crying from the sexual advances of his friend's older brother? Where was he when that young man was curled up in a ball, crying in guilt and shame for making himself cum? Where was God's mercy and understanding when that young man went to his minister, asked for help, and was excommunicated from God's church for acting on his evil desires? And most of all, where the fuck were you, God, when my father was fucking another woman and my mother was curled up in a ball, crying in guilt and shame as if she had done something wrong. Where were you? You fucking Supreme Asshole!

By the time I arrived at my apartment, my eyes were red with lack of sleep and my face wet with tears of anguish. I pulled into my parking stall, put my car in neutral, left it running, and put my head in my folded arms on my steering wheel.

Is there such a being as a God? If there is, does he love me? Or is he pissed off because I am abusing myself by abusing his daughters? For the first time in my life, I contemplated running a hose from the exhaust to the interior of my car to prepare myself to meet this elusive being. The thought didn't last too long however, as memories of the pair of lips he had blessed one of his daughters with came to my mind and began to release life-preserving pheromones from my brain. I wasn't about to take a chance of never feeling those blessed lips sucking my blood filled penis again. I knew angels had wings, but did they have dicks? And if they did, did God allow them to get head? I wasn't about to find out.

I got out of my car and went into my apartment. Once inside, I gathered up the clothes that I had angrily thrown all over my bedroom. I glanced at the clock and realized I only had a couple more hours before I had to leave to pick up Marlee. I took off my underwear, threw it in the clothes hamper, and headed for the shower. In the shower, my ritual went as it always does, filled with the search for self-approval and self-realization.

Before leaving my apartment, I checked it out for any semblance of "expecting a woman over." I went back to my bedroom, opened the clothes hamper, and pulled out an armful of clothes. I brought them into the living room and tossed them haphazardly in a pile. This action would come in handy later.

On the way to Marlee's house I glanced at my sparkling eyes in the rear view mirror. "Are you sure you want to start something with a virgin?" I questioned myself. Virgins are very susceptible to the natural enticings of the sex drive. Each new experience opens a whole new world of uncharted sexual pleasure. The wrong kind of man can ruin a virgin for life. Virgins are like thoroughbred horses—when they are young, each movement towards them, each caress of their mane, the way the bit is placed in their mouth and the saddle strapped on determines how well that horse is going to behave when ridden. If one jumps on that horse and kicks the shit out of it in a show of supremacy and control, that horse will never be any better than a farm plow horse. To make it a true racehorse that will have the endurance and capabilities to bring its owner success and pleasure in future races, it has to be trained properly with patience and persistence.

A woman usually learns her sexual habits and procedures from the first man that she has an ongoing sexual relationship with. An experienced man can tell how well a woman's previous sex partner performed during the first time he is with her. If a woman had a bad sexual experience from her mentor, she is easily responsive to the physical seductions and manipulations of a master.

Women fantasize about the perfect man and how he should make love to her. When her expectations are not met during sex, she is unresponsive and semicomatose in her movements and expression of pleasure. Though this woman might experience a climax of a physical and emotional release, she still hasn't experienced a real orgasm.

These women are like putty in the hands of a master. A man who knows what he is doing fulfills all the fantasized expectations that a woman has dreamed about. With every move of his hands, his tongue, and his torso, he sends pulsating energy through every nerve cell in her body.

After experiencing sex with a master, it is hard for a woman to revert back to the inexperience or lack of control of a man who has no idea what he is doing. That's exactly why the religions of men have come up with the commandments of men.

Men realize that if a studlier male comes along and entices his woman to sleep with him, she will never go back to her original mate. The commandments are set up to protect men's manhood and assure that he doesn't lose his property to someone else. The big diamond ring is also an indication of a male's insecurity about himself. The more visible the diamond, the less enticing the woman should appear to possible competition.

You see, men are more worried about their size than women are. The reason why we have no problem seeing two women together, or may even get excited to contemplate a threesome with two women, is because another woman is not a threat to our manliness—she doesn't have a dick! But, if our woman suggests a threesome with another man, we get all flustered and angry, and can't believe she would even think of such a thing. Players on the other hand, are very secure in their manhood and know how to use any tool that is at their disposal, regardless of its size, to accomplish the task of giving pleasure to a woman.

I knew that when the time came for Marlee to be introduced into the world of ultimate ecstasy, I would have to use all the patience of a world-class horse breeder and the finesse of a certified, experienced Player. If I was going to take the time to train her, I wanted her to become the best ride I ever had. And remembering the races I have participated in, I had a lot of training to do.

I arrived at Marlee's home around 6:55, five minutes before the expected time of my arrival. The worst thing a Player can do is play the games that other men play. Men love to make women wait for them and anticipate their grand entrance. Men believe that by being late, they are not showing too much anxiousness in wanting to get into a woman's pants. Women can be late, but they want their men to be on time and show that they are eager to see them. I always arrive early to show my respect, responsibility, and eagerness to see a woman. This makes her feel good, and is an important step in foreplay.

The best lesson that a man can learn is that foreplay starts with the date proposal. A woman uses the time away from a man thinking about what kind of man he is, how he is going to treat her, and what his true intentions are. Men use this time to think of ways to get her to fuck him. The proper foreplay is to do things the way a woman wants. Arriving slightly early is what a woman wants.

I pulled into Marlee's driveway and noticed that she was not raised in poverty. I had gotten the first impression that she was well taken care of, but I didn't expect such an opulent residence. I got out of my car and adjusted my jacket so that it covered the right areas that would surely be noticed and inspected by her curious parents. I walked to the front door and rang the doorbell.

The door opened to the revelation of a mother that was a bit intimidated and curious. From her facial expression, I realized that Marlee had told them the truth about how and where we had met. A lot of women that live with their parents usually do not tell their parents much about the men that they date, knowing that Mom and Dad are very judgmental and leery of any man who wants part of their flesh and blood. Knowing that Marlee had told the truth, I instantly realized how to play her parents and the game began:

"Wow! Now I see where your daughter got her looks!" I eagerly said without a second's hesitation. Marlee's mother was indeed well endowed and held her breasts properly positioned for an older lady. Of course, my eyes never left hers. I smiled a warm smile and ended the mother's intimidation with the perpetual "mother's line":

"If you are any indication of what your daughter is going to look like in the future, then I am glad to meet you, Mom!" I confidently added, never wavering in my fixation on her eyes and keeping a continuous smile. (This comment is perpetual because mothers never get tired of hearing it.) With that said, the mother gave me the, "Oh, aren't you charming" response, and invited me into the house. Having the mother answer the door was another indication that Marlee knew very little about me when she told her parents she was going out tonight.

When her father came out of his in-house office, I had no doubt she had argued with him about going out with a stranger she had just met. Her father's eyes met mine with that father's stare that said, "Man to man, I know you want to fuck my daughter just like I wanted to fuck her mother when I first met her, so who the hell are you, thinking you can do what I did?"

"Hello, Sir!" I said. Calling a man "Sir" helps maintain the appropriate protocol that he is in control and respected by a lesser dick. I offered my hand without wavering from the smile that I had greeted his wife with. I knew he was much more hardened than his feminine sidekick, so I proceeded cautiously.

"So, what kind of work do you do?" he ordered.

I reached in my pocket to produce a business card as I explained the purpose of my work and the success I enjoyed in it. The business card is all the credentials that one needs to exude a sense of responsibility and professionalism.

"I can see that you probably won't be in need of my services owing to your obvious financial success. But in case a need arises, I am the best around," I confidently continued.

It wasn't too long after first meeting her father that Marlee appeared on the scene, still in the process of putting on her earrings. She smiled at me, said hello, then lost the smile and looked at her father. She passed by him, turned to her mother and kissed her, and said that she would be back later. She wasn't about to give her father any opportunity to get off the hook, so she avoided kissing him and didn't even look at him as she headed towards the front door, grabbing my hand on the way out.

This was my opportunity to impress the father and do a little more foreplay. I firmly held her hand and gently swung her back around to face her father.

"If my daughter was going out with a man that she just met today and knew nothing about, I would be a little concerned as to where they were going and what they were going to do," I offered.

Her father's head lifted up a little and Marlee stood there somewhat surprised, but submissive to my subtle control. I proceeded to inform her parents where we were going and tell them that I had tried to get their daughter to invite them to come with us; but she didn't want to see them kissing in the backseat while we were trying to engage in constructive conversation in the front. This humor made all three of them laugh and ended the tension.

After a little more humor and a bit of reassurance, Marlee left my side, hugged her father, and told him not to worry. Little did her father realize that the hug he was receiving was the last innocence he would ever experience from a daughter who was getting ready to become an experienced woman.

I had won the father's confidence and her trust, thus becoming the one to experience her. She would never really tell her father when and with whom she lost her virginity. She had told him not to worry. She certainly didn't want him to ever believe that she was wrong.

How could she have been wrong?

A Master of the Art

I opened the passenger side door so that she could get in my car. She got in and leaned over to my door to make sure it was unlocked. (A good sign that she was an experienced dater at least.) She smiled at me when I got in the driver's side and complimented me on the way I treated her parents. I made her put her seat belt on, and we went to a local bookstore that had a café incorporated in it for convenience.

When we arrived, I opened her door and let her out. She grabbed my hand (a sure sign that she liked what was happening) and led me toward the entrance. I stopped a short distance from the car and told her that my jacket was probably going to be a little too warm for the ambient temperature of the store.

I was probably wasting time by bearing my ass to her, because I knew she was intensely attracted to me. The rest of the way into the bookstore she held my right hand with her left hand, and looped her right arm through mine, snuggling those fine breasts right up next to my side. I knew she wanted me to feel them through her tight, knitted sweater, so I indulged myself by slightly turning into her as we walked.

Inside, we sat at a cozy table and started talking about previous relationships. I found that she was very particular as to whom she dated, and that she had found it virtually impossible to find the right mix of man, money, and motivation—the 3 M's that mean marriageable. It took me about 10 minutes to know exactly what I had to do to get down her shirt that night. I told her of the frustration and broken heart that I experienced with my last relationship, and emotionally demonstrated the lie by hanging my head and looking morosely to the side at times. She grabbed my hand from across the table and expressed her sympathy, but emphasized her gladness that there were guys who could truly express their feelings and emotions in a tender way. The hook was firmly set by now, and I was reeling her in.

After walking around the bookstore for a while, and demonstrating my unique ability to converse on just about any subject that we passed on the bookshelf, I knew it was time to make my move. During our excursion through the aisles of the bookstore, Marlee would caress my arms and side with her breasts. This was a safe way for her to be petted. After each hour, the caressing got more forward and specific. At one point her eyes caught mine, and for that moment a window of opportunity opened for me to kiss her.

Patience was indeed needed in this situation if I was going to get that sweater off of her tonight. So I didn't even give a slight indication that I wanted to kiss her. This made her want to kiss me even more. She was accustomed to the "boys" she had dated wanting to kiss her as soon as she allowed it. What she wasn't accustomed to was the touch of a man's hands on her breasts tenderly caressing them and exciting the nipples to erection and pleasure. She was going to experience both tonight.

We sat back down inside the café part of the bookstore at about 10 PM. We had been out for three hours, had had stimulating conversation and deep stares of romance, and not once had I tried to kiss her or make any movements that she had to withdraw from. She was impressed—I was playing her.

"Well, it's probably getting close to your curfew and I don't want your dad to think I want to take advantage of his daughter, so I better get you home," I said almost concerned.

"I'm 26 years old and don't have a curfew!" she shot back frustrated. It was just the frustration I was looking for.

"Okay. That means you must enjoy my company," I smiled.

She affirmed what I already knew. I explained to her that I usually feel a little uncomfortable having someone that I barely know over to my small apartment, and that it certainly wasn't in any condition to accept company. But if she wanted to come over and watch a movie with me, and if she could ignore the pile of unwashed clothes in the living room, she was welcome to come.

I hadn't made any advances toward her the whole evening. She never caught me staring at her boobs or looking at other women—this made her feel comfortable. The fact that I had a load of dirty laundry in my front room gave the impression that I certainly wasn't planning on having her come over to my apartment on our first date—this brought her into the light. I was mature and responsible in the way I treated her parents—this flipped her into my boat.

When we reached my apartment complex, Marlee was a bit curious as to why we had to park so far away from my front door when there was an empty spot right in front of the building where my apartment was located. I explained to her that one of the other occupants in my building was expecting a child any time, and that all of the residents got together and dedicated that particular parking stall—which I so graciously offered—to the expectant mother. After a brief outburst of accolades and thankfulness that she finally had found a truly caring person to date, she put her arms around me and attempted to kiss me. I turned my face, kissed her cheek, and thanked her for her compliments.

We entered my apartment and I invited her to make herself at home. She followed me into the living room where we ran into the pile of dirty clothes on the floor. I picked them up and excused myself so that I could put them back into the dirty clothes hamper where they had come from just hours before.

When I returned to the living room, she was admiring the assortment of books on my bookshelves and commented on the fact that she felt a little intimidated by how well read I was. I asked her if she had read any of the works that I had available. She said that she had heard of most of them, but had limited knowledge in their writings.

"What about art?" I asked.

I took her over to the few abstract prints I had hanging on the wall. Her blank expression told me that she had no idea what she was looking at. This was the first time that I made any physical motion toward her. I came up behind her and put my hands on her shoulders, slightly massaging them and relating the intention of the art piece before her.

"This artist lived during the great depression and was greatly affected by the poverty and living conditions of the people of America. He longed to make a difference by relating his feelings in his art work."

"Do you see the way these lines are running horizontally through the whole piece?" I asked as I moved my body closer to hers and I reached to follow the horizontal lines that I knew absolutely nothing about. My chest was pressed firmly against her back and my penis sensed the outline of her buttocks. I felt her neck relax and her head fall gently against my chest as I swept my arm in front of her traversing the imaginary line that I was making up. My arm brushed the front section of her breasts and I felt her inhale softly.

After my pointed finger reached the side of the painting, I dropped my hands to her upper arms and held them gently. She continued to lay her head in my chest and I began a gentle massage of her upper arms. With each outward stroke, my knuckles would caress the sides of her breasts. My head was above hers and I began to notice her hardening nipples protruding through her size Triple D bra and her sweater. God, they were beautiful!

I proceeded to tell her some more made up bullshit about the intent of an artist I had imagined up, all the while continuing my gentle massage movements and outer caressing of her breasts. I felt her breathing increase with each pass of my knuckles and noticed her eyelids fall shut. Her nostrils flared out, and her respiration increase was obvious fi om the in and out motion of her flat stomach. Now she was in the hands of the fisherman, totally unaware of her fate in this new world of light that he had pulled her into.

I slowly placed my face against the side of hers. She responded the same way a newborn responds to a gentle caress on its cheek—it moves its face toward the stimulant and attempts to suck on it. Marlee's lips were red and full with blood. Slightly open, she moved her mouth toward my cheek. She held her warm, moist lips next to my cheek and gently moaned. I slowly moved my lips towards hers. Her lips left a wet pathway on my face. I took her lips in mine and gently kissed them. Her small moans became more intense and wanting. She kept her mouth slightly opened and I caressed her lower lip with my soft tongue. Her eyes were still closed and her body began to tremble slightly.

I turned her body towards mine and began to kiss her passionately. What she didn't notice was that as I turned her body towards me, my hand found one of her breasts, and I gently held it in my cupped hand. The kissing was the distraction that made the placement of my hand seem comfortable and a natural move. Though the energy of my touch had to permeate a sweater and a reinforced bra, she could feel the desire.

As the kissing became more intense, my thumb and index finger found her erect nipple and rolled it slightly upwards. My other hand was gently supporting the back of her head, my thumb smoothly caressing the soft erotic zone just behind her ear. Our breathing quickened and became a musical symphony of rhythm and beats. Each note rang clear from the instrument that was playing it. Each stanza's crescendo reaching higher notes than the one before.

I knew that if I went much further at this time I could ruin the natural comfort level that I had carefully developed. With this thought, I withdrew my lips slightly from hers. By now her lips were filled with blood—soft, passionate pillows of lust ready to accept whatever I wanted to give them. A soft sigh came out of her mouth when we separated, which paused the orchestrated melody.

"I'm sorry," I whispered, moving my hand away from her breast area in hopes that my supplication for forgiveness would convince her that it was something that had "just happened" in the heat of passion. My body stayed firmly entwined in hers, but my hand never left the cradle position where it rocked a soft neck and hairline of a needy baby. And what came next didn't surprise me at all.

Marlee moved back slightly and looked up longingly into my eyes. She smiled slightly and reached behind her. Both of her hands disappeared under her sweater and up her back. How they do it is a mystery many men have futilely tried to solve—she unfastened her bra with one quick motion.

She brought her hands back in front of her and gently grabbed my left hand and guided it under her sweater until it found one of the firmest natural breasts I had ever felt. Her bra was hiding more than appeared through her clothes. My hand could not hold all of her breast at once. It softly explored the untouched regions of her breasts in awe at the rush of discovering uncharted territory. My exploration ended when her erect nipple entered the valley I had formed between my thumb and index finger. My fingers were trained and knew exactly what they needed to do to create a volcano of emotion out of that mountain peak, and cause lava to flow freely at its base.

Marlee threw her head back, grabbed my hand outside her sweater, and moaned as she moved it from one breast to the other. Her knees quivered for a moment and she rested herself against the painting hanging on the wall. I moved more to the side, brought her body closer to mine, and found her pulsating lips ready to engulf my own as soon as they were near.

Gently, I lowered her to the ground and cradled her in my arms, my hand still stimulating the volcanic reaction that I was sure had the lava flowing strongly in her panties. Our kissing once again became passionate—reaching and surpassing the previous crescendo we had attained.

She lay there totally under my control. Her body quivered with desire—her heart beating faster, her breathing increasing.

My hand left the now extremely hard nipple and slowly rubbed her tight stomach. My fingers slightly passed the boundaries of her jeans and I felt the top few pubic hairs that led to the warm lava pit. She could sense my desire to push my hand down her pants and feel her wetness. I waited to see if she would respond—my hand finding her nipple again, agitating the lava flow.

My lips left hers and found the spot behind her ear that my fingers had seductively prepared. I kissed her gently and licked her softly. She was hypnotized. The pheromones in her body engulfed the parts of her brain that helped her think clearly. Her hands found the buttons on her jeans and with little effort opened them up. She took my hand again and helped it find what we both desired.

She was so wet. The cum flowed freely over my fingers as they explored another region where no man had ever journeyed. With each gentle stroke, she raised her hips slightly, longing for my fingers to penetrate her.

Some might call it an epiphany. I call it a distraction. But whatever one might call it, it still had a profound effect on me at that moment. It was as if someone had turned on a vacuum, put it up to my ear, and sucked every last drop of sexual hormones out of my body. I was limper than an overcooked Oscar Meyer.

I took my hand away from Marlee and lay down near her without touching her. I was astonished by my inability to finish what I had started. There by my side laid the epitome of innocence—a virgin, previously untouched by any other man. I was the fisherman playing with the fish that I had caught. First I admired its beauty and held it out of water for longer than usual as I turned it over and over looking for any imperfection that would force me to throw it back. I couldn't find any.

Who am I? What right do I have to take advantage of the trust of this woman? Everything I told her, everything I did up to this point, had been an orchestrated lie—a deception used many times before to reach this desired situation. What! Was my conscious, which lay dormant for so long, finally surfacing and making me face the fact that I was a selfish bastard whose only desire was to make himself feel good?

The gasps of the fish I held grew deeper and more wanting as I kept it in my hands, unable to decide whether to throw it back or put it in my fish bag where it would join the other dead fish, and eventually die of suffocation itself.

When my father had an affair on my mother, was she innocent and unknowing? Was she trusting and confidant of the love that my father was supposed to have for her? In her final gasps of air that caused her to leave her children, did he have the compassion to let her live again? Or did he want her to die, so that he could prove that he had won the fight and earned the trophy?

When my mother confronted him about the affair, he had lied and told her she was crazy. I was three years old. I didn't know if my mother was crazy. But when she left work one day to pick me up from school because the pre-school teacher couldn't get a hold of my father at his job, and carried me into the house; was she crazy for hearing the moaning and groaning from the upstairs bedroom?

She might have been as crazy as my father had always told us she was. But I wasn't. When my mother threw open the bedroom door, I say my father on top of my babysitter—a virgin. I wasn't crazy when I felt the bump on my head caused by my mother dropping me and collapsing herself in tears and anguish. I wasn't crazy when I heard my father attempt to justify what he was doing, further agonizing my mother. I wasn't crazy when they both left the room yelling at each other, my mother crying profusely and my father calling her a bitch.

And that other girl. What made her think that she could put on her panties, pick me up, and attempt to calm my shattered heart? That was the first and the last time that I ever hit a woman in the face with my hand. I wasn't crazy, when for the second time I felt a bump on my head when the babysitter dropped me.

The fish was taking its final breaths when my dick began to get hard again.

I rolled back over onto Marlee and passionately kissed her again. This time I was in control and she was mine. I hid the tears in my eyes with the sound of my voice resonating that I wanted her then and now. My tongue found her breasts and I lapped ferociously at the erect nipples. My head went lower and found her wet vagina pulsating at the sexual dance it had just experienced. My lips found the outer portions of her vagina and played them with a composition that Mozart would have been embarrassed by.

In her last breaths, the fish could be heard crying for its master to put it out of its misery. Marlee couldn't stand the passion any longer and her standing ovation let me know that she was ready for the last big blast from the orchestra.

I pulled her pants the rest of the way off and tore mine down to my knees. This fish was mine. I was the master who had reeled her in and won the fight. I bashed her head up against the boat to silence her—I fucked Marlee harder than I had ever fucked any other woman. She was no longer a virgin—she was dead! And I? I was a fisherman, just like my fucking father.

Professional Stamina

I took Marlee home that evening in virtual silence. When we reached her driveway, she broke the silence with a phrase that all Player's dread, but have the experience and expertise to answer without hesitation:

"So, what does this mean?" she quietly inquired.

After receiving me in such a hard, fast manner, she was definitely sore, but bled surprisingly very little. The foreplay had created such a tremendous amount of lubrication that she took me with quite a bit of ease. I didn't notice how tight she probably was due to my emotional state at the time. I know she didn't arrive at an orgasm, and mine was affected by my emotions and barely satisfied my manly needs.

We lay together afterwards, and I distantly heard the same words that I have heard many times before: That I was wonderful. That she had never felt anything like it. That she felt so incredibly close to me. That she hoped that I understood that I meant a lot to her demonstrated by the fact that she let me sleep with her.

Let me sleep with her? I had her under my power and she was helpless to stop me. She told me how often she had thought about letting a man have sex with her, but that I was someone she truly thought she could love and have a relationship with, and that's why she felt so comfortable about letting me be the first. Please! Spare me from more of this female co-dependency bullshit that I call love.

Without responding to her hypnotic gestures, I glanced hurriedly at the clock and told her we had to get her home at a reasonable time so that "Dad" wouldn't hate me. How nice! I was calling her dad my dad. How reassuring for a woman to hear this and believe that this man could possibly be the one that would call her father "Dad" forever.

"It means that I can't wait to see you again, and hope that my sexual aggression can be forgiven. I have never had sex on the first date," I lied.

I stopped the car, gently leaned over toward her, and tenderly grabbed the back of her head. Her eyes met mine and longingly stared at me, hoping for more reassurance that what we had done was the right thing.

"I've never felt this way before. I've always looked for someone like you. I have feelings that I haven't felt for a long, long time," I continued my lie. "Don't worry about losing me. This is a start of a beautiful relationship."

The latter was probably closer to the truth than anything else I had said during the evening. She did have at least 4 to 6 months.

Marlee buried her head in my shoulder and whimpered like a puppy dog just purchased by a little boy who never had one before. We kissed gently one more time before I walked her to her front door and embraced her for the final time that evening. The front porch light miraculously came on, so we both knew Mom and Dad were watching.

Back in my car, I had regained my emotional control and tried to figure out if I had received any satisfaction out of the night's events. Well, it didn't matter anyway. My night was just beginning. I was on my way to see Victoria.

I was not planning to have sex with Marlee on the first date—believing that it was going to be a little harder than it actually was to seduce her. Maybe I underestimated my own skills. Victoria's lips were going to be the climax of the evening. Of all the women I have been with, very few can make me cum by giving me head—Victoria could accomplish the task anytime she wanted.

On my way to Victoria's, I called her to let her know my business meeting was over and I was on my way. After having sex with Marlee, I carefully washed myself with soap and water making sure no lingering smell was present from the ordeal. Women can smell another woman a mile away. The perfect solution for a Player is to wear an after-shave or cologne that is stronger than a woman's perfume. This masks any sense of femininity that might be a residue from being with another woman.

I made it to Victoria's house around 1 am, and found her rested and ready for me. I mentioned how tired I was from the late meeting but that I was glad I was finally in her arms. She laid me down on her bed, slowly undressed me, and massaged my body.

Finally her clothes came off and her lips took over where her hands had been. She kissed every part of my body until she came to the organ that brought us both exquisite pleasure. When she was finished, we both laid back gasping for air.

She laid her head on my shoulder and whispered the words that I had heard once before that evening. She was pleased with what I gave to her, and I was pleased with what she gave to me. One couldn't ask for a more giving relationship.

"I doubt I will ever meet anyone that can take your place, my sweet Victoria," I reassured her.

It was true. No one would ever take her place, but she would soon be replaced as soon as the novelty of her lips wore off. If a man finds a women that totally satisfies him in every way sexually, there is a good possibility that he will keep her around, possibly for life. He will be satisfied with the one-night stands he can squeeze in on business trips and daytime excursions, but he will make a really great sex partner his companion, his wife, or whatever she has to be called to make her feel that she's his only one.

I laid with Victoria until about 5:00 AM. She was asleep, so I gently kissed her ear and whispered that I had to get home and do some laundry before starting work the next day. She quietly moaned and smiled, reaching up to brush my hair, thus giving me her approval that she was okay with me leaving. Like I really needed her approval.

The fact is, Players don't like the idea too much of staying over at one of their woman's houses. It becomes uncomfortable, because he begins to sense that the woman possesses him too much for the situation. Furthermore, he hates seeing what the woman really looks like in the morning, and would rather avoid the disappointment. If he wanted to put up with a droopy face, smeared mascara, and morning breath, he would get married, now wouldn't he?

I left Victoria's and felt fulfilled and peaceful as I drove to my own small, comfortable apartment. I parked my car where it was supposed to be parked and went inside.

I took more clothes out of the hamper and threw them in piles all over the front room and kitchen. I washed the glass Marlee had used to get a drink of water and put it back in the cupboard. These rituals are simple habits that I have developed over the years, and for good reason.

I was pretty tired at this point and went straight to bed without brushing my teeth, something I normally would never do.

Ahhhhh...finally alone in my queen-sized bed. It was dark in my apartment and I listened to the silence of the still air that surrounded me. I was home. This was my domain. It existed for and because of me. It was my haven, my safe house away from the world. Only I had a key to my apartment and I would never let a woman have a copy. The phone could ring, the door could be knocking, but in my domain I choose to be alone or not. Yet, I realized that I would have to answer the phone or door if either happened, because I had parked my car in its rightful place.

I stayed awake for a time staring into the darkness recounting the activities of earlier in the evening. Marlee's breasts were amazing. Her desire and passion were intense, and her first experience of intercourse a success, at least for her.

Victoria's lips were incredible as usual, and the orgasm we shared made up for the one that was hidden behind the hurt and anger I was feeling when I came into Marlee. I was satisfied.

I began to get hard again, so I turned over in an effort to stop thinking about women. On my side I noticed a faint light from the outside flicker on the white wall. It was caused by the tree limbs outside of my window blowing in the wind and letting through rays of light from the parking lot lights. The light danced on my wall and I imagined a little fairy doing a dance for me in an attempt to seduce me. She flirted with the darkness with tiny steps that took her from side to side. She seemed to be beckoning me to come and dance with her.

For a moment my mind floated over to the wall and I became a being of light also. I took her small hand in mine and flirted with the dance that she had begun. I smiled at my little image of light dancing on that wall, and found myself lulled to sleep by my imaginary seductress.

A knocking at my door and the ringing of my doorbell startled me. I woke up and found that the tiny silhouette dancer had been replaced with the strong rays of her father, the morning sun. I looked at my clock and found that I had soundly slept until 9 AM.

"Who the hell is that?" I asked myself as I stumbled out of bed.

I went to the door and peered through the eyehole. There was Amy, wide-eyed and bushy-tailed, holding an espresso and a muffin—my favorite kind, of course.

I knew my car was parked where it was supposed to be, so I had no excuse not to answer the door. I quickly glanced behind me and analyzed the situation knowing that I was prepared for this unexpected visit. Thank God for my developed habits and Player's intuition.

"Hey, Baby!" I said as I opened the door. "What a surprise."

Amy knew that we would be together tonight, but she also realized that I had just endured a long night of meetings, and she stopped by on her way to work to remind me of what I was going to receive that evening.

I realized that I hadn't showered from the episode with Victoria, so I protected her advances toward me by claiming I wanted to jump in the shower quickly and brush my teeth. She threw her arms around me anyway and pushed her groin next to mine. I looked down behind her and saw that gorgeous ass that I could never refuse. I hardened up faster than 2-second epoxy.

"So you do want me," she said sheepishly attempting to get further acknowledgment that I had given.

I offered the best fake moan I could muster and told her to get her gorgeous body naked and get it in my bed. I excused myself to my bathroom and quickly brushed my teeth and washed the residue of Victoria down the drain—there went my emotions again.

When I crawled in my bed on top of Amy, I could feel the incredible wetness she had created between her legs. I flipped her over on top of me, then stayed hard and ready as she performed the incredible ballet that a hard ass and slim waste can master. She came about 6 times before laying her body on top of my wet chest—the wetness was all from her own cum—letting me know that it was my turn.

My turn? I had just had my turn twice in the last 12 hours. Did I have another turn left in me? I reached behind Amy, grabbed her incredible butt, and felt the moisture and heat permeating between her hard cheeks. You bet I do. And I did.

Hidden Remorse

Amy quickly rinsed off in my shower, gave me a kiss, and walked that perfect ass out of my apartment to go to work.

I lay in bed, a little amazed at my ability to screw three different women in half a day. I smiled and patted myself on the back with the thought. How many men would love to be in my position—the best tits, lips, and ass anyone could hope for.

Some might think I should feel guilty for what I am doing to these women. What exactly am I doing to these women? I am nice to them, I wine them, I dine them, I give them the compliments that each want. I am a companion to them; I listen to their complaints and trials that they experience in life; and most of all, I satisfy them sexually in every way. So what am I doing except giving them exactly what they want?

Yea, yea, I know. I am not giving them what they really want. They want love. In other words, co-dependency. They want to believe that they are special and chosen above all other women to stand by my side and fulfill my desires. They want to believe that I am faithful to them in every way and that I think about them as much as they think about me. They want security and loyalty, trust, and compassion. They want a man.

Now, most women are a bit different than most men. Women give sex to get love, and men love to get sex. What does this mean, Ladies? It means that even though we say we love you, we just want to fuck you. And Gentlemen, you better be aware that if she lets you fuck her, she wants you to love her too.

Women have brought this dilemma on themselves. You make us do all the horseshit that we have to do to entice you to sleep with us. In other words, you make us court you and prove that we love you, and make you think you are special before we are allowed the opportunity to have sex with you. Owing to this, of course, we are going to lie to you. We can't love you the way you want us to; we are men. We love like men, act like men, and fuck like men. You ladies are women. You love like women, act like women, and won't allow yourself to be fucked unless you're treated like women.

Do you think we are stupid, Ladies? Do you think we like giving up our freedom, our money, our time, and our possessions to a woman? What do you think we get out of it? Do you think we get freedom, money, time, and possessions from you? Do you think men look at women and say, "Oh, I wonder what kind of car she drives and what kind of job she has?" Hell, no! We want to see what you got under those jeans, behind that bra, and how you use them to please our dicks. We get nothing from you but sex. And if you don't give us what we desire, fuck you, we'll find it somewhere else. And when we go looking somewhere else, you sit there and sulk and rage and figure out every way you can make us hurt as much as you are hurting. Men move on. Women hold on.

Nothing is greater than the wrath of a woman scorned. Oh, the wisdom in this statement. Women cannot accept the fact that her man is not satisfied with her and will make sure he is fucked in one way or another if he isn't fucking her.

Nevertheless Gentlemen, we have a safeguard that to some degree, alleviates a woman's wrath. It's called the other woman. No woman wants to admit to herself that another woman is better than she is. So, when papa moves on to a different mama, the woman puts a lot, if not all, the blame on the whore who stole her man. Ladies, why can't you just accept the fact that you suck in bed, your butt got flabby and fat, and your man is moving on to greener pastures. If you are so worried about the grass on the other side of the fence, then water yours, trim it, fertilize it, and make it comfortable for your man to play in it. Get it through your heads that we are men, we want sex, and that is really all we get from you. We give things to get, and you get things so that you will give. It's that simple.

Being a Player is much safer for a man than a regular monogamous relationship, which in reality does not even exist. Admittedly, there are men that do not cheat on their wives or girlfriends; but if they had the chance and could justify it in some way, they would—it's in our nature. The Player's ability to charm and treat a woman like she wants to be treated guarantees him sex. His inability to make a commitment to any one woman guarantees him financial and emotional freedom. Some Players find a woman who is extraordinary in bed, and might even consider marriage, if the woman expects that commitment in return for her service. But she would have to be really good and kind of dumb, because he will definitely participate in extramarital affairs, and therefore needs a woman who he can manipulate and deceive easily.

I often wonder why women get so bent out of shape (besides eating too much) over men and their polygamous natures. Thousands of years ago our ancestors certainly did not form unions as we do today.

The female species of most primate societies are the caring, nurturing, and responsible party in most cases. Her only desire is to care for herself and her young ones. The males fight with each other over who gets to have sex with the females. A stronger male usually wins out and drives the weaker ones away. Obviously, the males are naturally pursuing what they desire. What else are they good for?

Well, it seems reasonable that some of the females decided that it was impossible for one male to care for all those females and their needs. So females began to break off from the group and stand-alone. Pretty soon one female had other males coming up to her and offering her food and protection, if she would have sex with them. Now, it is illogical to assume that the male was offering food and protection because he was a "nice guy." He wanted to have sex and saw the offerings as a way of getting it.

It soon became apparent to the "stand-alone" female and her new mate, that if he would take care of her needs, she would give him sex whenever he wanted—a win-win situation. If another male came along and wanted the female, he would have to prove a better mate than her present, but if her present was faithfully providing for all of her needs, she would find no need to allow the new pursuer an opportunity to have sex with her.

Thus began the codependency between a male and a female. In other words, thus began LOVE.

There would be no room for handsome Players in a society where all the males generally looked alike, as in other primate families, and where there was an equal portion of males to females. However, human men must be men. So we go to war and kill each other, get thrown in jail for being men, and find that other men can give us just as much pleasure, and maybe even more, than a woman. (The first thing a single woman says when she sees a gorgeous man who is single is, "He's probably gay." Did you ever wonder Ladies, why so many of us are turning gay? Because most of you are bitches who want what we got without giving what we need. So there!)

What did I ever get from the women that my father brought into my life after my mother left? Sure, they clothed me, they fed me, they made me do chores, and they watched out for me. But did they ever give me what I really needed? Did they ever hold me tenderly after I skinned a knee and tell me how much they loved me? Did they care enough to wonder why I was crying late at night when they yelled for me to shut up through the darkness?

There on my wall, as a child, I saw the light fairy dancing through my tears. I cried silently, hoping that my father's partner wouldn't hear me and get upset. The fairy would calm my troubled soul and lull me to sleep. When I awoke, she was gone. But I knew she would be back—back to love me like I wanted to be loved. I didn't have to give to her to get. She was my mother.

Anyway, back to what women want from us—there are many, many single women looking for the "right" man. Most of the men that they meet are certainly not the "right" man. A Player can become the "right" man to any woman he chooses, and with this ability, his basket is always full of eager women wanting to have sex with him.

So why should I be sorry that I am a Player? I give a woman what she wants, and she gives me what I want. We are both pleased. Yea, yea, again I know—a woman wants loyalty and faithfulness and commitment (a four letter word to a Player—LOVE). And Players lie about their ability to provide any of these things. True it might be, but at the moment I am with a woman, I treat her as if she is the only one. And as long as I provide her with the food and protection that she desires, why should she care what I am doing outside of her cave?

Men act like men because women force us to. Can you imagine a man being totally honest with a woman? Hey, Baby, you're looking fine tonight! Would you like to fuck after I take you to dinner once or twice, buy you a few things, tell you that you're beautiful, and praise your family?

Women cannot accept that we are who we are, so they will always be putting us down and ridiculing our natural behavior. Players simply prey on a woman being a woman. To get rid of Players, you have to get rid of women. In truth, we would probably have a better world if, at least in the sex department, women acted more like men.

Well, I got it out. The preceding outburst of feminine insolence is usually what goes through my mind when sympathetic feelings of remorse creep in trying to persuade me that I should end my playing and give a woman what she really wants from a man.

My drains are well vented and clean. Every shower, every day, washes the residue of the women I play down these disposal avenues. Diluted and dissolved by soaps and shampoos, their memories are quickly washed away—forgotten and hidden—just like my emotions.

Proper Management

Remember the fish philosopher and what he said, "If it looks too good to be true, it probably isn't?" Luckily for Players, women refuse to accept this sagacious warning. Women are dreamers. They read too many romance novels—which, by the way, are mostly written by women—they watch too many soap operas, and are brainwashed by the "chick flicks" that Hollywood masterly creates for them. They believe that one day, and any day will do, they will find "The One."

"The One" is the epitome of what a man should be. When a man figures out what should is, he will be able to control the woman and be "The One." Control—this is the only way a Player can make sure his women are satisfied and unaware of each other.

A good memory is essential in order for a man to control his relationships and actions towards his women. Anyone who uses a day planner probably doesn't have the best memory, and is probably one that is easily controlled instead of being controlling. The planner controls his or her daily activities. On the other hand, an individual who stores all of his or her activities in their natural day planner, or brain, is in control of him or herself, and needs no outside source to control his or her time.

I haven't written down a woman's phone number in years. As soon as I am told a number, I automatically store it in my memory bank by association. When Victoria whispered her phone number to me on the dance floor, I immediately placed it under 5 red cherries for a 7-inch squirrel that sits between 2 huge walnuts in a 69 position sucking 1 cherry then 2 cherries—her number is 572-6912.

One of the biggest mistakes a man can make is to write down the name and number of a girl and put it in his pocket. There have been many surprised wives and girlfriends who come across pieces of paper with phone numbers written on them. When I was in the early years, I would write down some numbers occasionally, but would always include a fictitious man's name next to the woman's so that if found, I would explain that, "This is one of my friends. He wants us to get together with him and his wife for drinks some night." Sometimes a business card can be logically explained away and would be a better way to take a woman's information. Nevertheless, to maintain solid control always, nothing is more efficient and safe than the enigmatic brain.

All women will thumb through your day planner or briefcase if given the chance. Anything written down is a liability to your game. Women, though easily manipulated, are not stupid. They have an inner intuition that aids them in smelling out the infidelity of their man. I think it was God's gift to Eve to keep Adam eating apples out of only her hand.

A Player learns about this intuition and stays one step ahead of it. All numbers need to be safely stored in an area hidden from the intuition and suspect of a woman—they cannot read minds.

With practice, a daily itinerary can be stored, rearranged, and followed in the memory banks of the brain. This ability distinguishes between an ordinary man and a Player.

The "right" man for a woman thinks only of her and plans his life around what she needs. And women can easily be convinced that she's the "only one." With no written evidence of what a man does, a woman accepts the hope that her man doesn't have the time, or the intelligence, to possibly come up with so many different appointments and late business meetings when she is inquiring as to why her man can't see her tonight. With the hope so conveniently inculcated into her mind by the media, she faithfully accepts her role as his "only one."

There hasn't been one woman in my life who has thought there was a possibility I was cheating on her. "Not, my man!" she boldly states. "My man is different. I know he doesn't cheat on me."

I set them up to believe this. The set-up is simple: Never, ever look at another woman when you are out with your victim. When another woman approaches or starts to flirt, be quick and to the point, but kind, and show no interest in the other woman. When your victim points out that another woman was attempting to flirt with you, act dumb and deny that any woman would try to flirt with you. Tell her that she needs to take a good look in the mirror and see what you see. What you see is a different woman than you have ever seen before. Ask her if she knows very many other women with the same traits and characteristics that she has. She'll think about it, but won't come up with any other.

Subtly point out and cut down the good points that other women have over your victim. If she has small boobs, tell her how disgusting it is to feel the hard, un-sensitive implants that most women get to enlarge their breasts. If she doesn't have much of a butt, tell her how you can't understand how other men can stand having all of that ass to contend with during sex. In other words, enhance her shortcomings by diminishing the enhancements. I swear, if all of my girls got together in one room (well, you better make that a city park), none of them would believe that I would have even been attracted to any other—a woman's inherent competition with other females makes my success even more possible.

A Player rarely calls his women by their first names—this is a dangerous practice. He uses "Baby," "Gorgeous," "Light of My Life," "Sweetie," and other meaningless pseudonyms that are normally accepted by those who want to think they are special. With this habit in place, a man never has to worry about calling a woman by the wrong name. One time while having sex with Amy, I inadvertently called her Judy. My quick tongue saved me this time as I finished the statement, "Oh God, Judy! Jew need! You need me, ahhhhhhhhhhhhh yes, Baby!" She never caught it.

Practice makes perfect. A Player's management skills are developed and refined over time. I could fill volumes with suggestions, come-on lines, and responses to different situations that arise when a man is playing a woman. The game is not a constant; its rules and structure continually change with each woman that is played. Adaptability is essential. And adaptability cannot be taught—it must be lived and learned through experience.

Proper management guarantees success. Success for a Player is the ability to adapt to any situation, so that he appears too good to be true, but all the same, he appears to be.

The Game Continues

On my way to work that morning, I realized that I had known Victoria for about 6 months, and the newness of her contribution to my sexual gratification was wearing off. Though I would miss her lips, Amy's butt and the intrigue of teaching Marlee the deep mysteries of Karma Sutra, would keep my interest satisfied until Victoria could be replaced.

I guess it isn't so much that teaching new things to a virgin intrigues me, but seeing her react to the new feelings and emotions that she is experiencing does. Nothing is more exciting than watching a woman's eyes as she experiences her first orgasm. Her eyes widen, her mouth falls open, and her thrusts become intense and strong. The release of energy leaves her breathless and totally bonded to the lover that introduced her to such ecstasy. The memories of her former boyfriends fade as the orgasmic juices of a "real" orgasm become acidic and wipe her sexual slate clean. She is now ready to experience sex in a whole new way. And he who made her feel this way has won her heart.

When a woman gives her heart to a man, she loses part of her personal control. It's this control that a man wants. Maybe when a man rapes a woman, he uses his stronger physical attributes to control the woman, thus proving to himself that he is a man. Or maybe it's just nature forcing him to do what he was created to do. Is the control that a man desires through rape that much different than the control he desires by winning a woman's heart? Perhaps when a woman is giving her heart freely, she is saying, "Here, take control of me. Make me miss you, want you, and need you. Control the very essence of who I am, so that when you leave, I am devastated."

Do I rape women? The thought has crossed my mind. A rapist has no intention of furthering the relationship with the woman he is forcing to give up her control. And I have no intention on having a long-term relationship with any woman I sleep with. Yet I love to control them. I want them to want me, miss me, need me, and be devastated when I leave the relationship. I manipulate them and lie to them to get them to believe that I care more about them than a rapist does about his victims.

I can't be a rapist. I have never forced myself on a woman. Hell, I usually let the woman make the first move towards physical affection. This patience makes them yearn to kiss me. I use my techniques to entice them, perhaps control them, but they want everything I give them, so force is not necessary. Maybe the trauma of the experience is the same, but whose fault is that?

Like many times before, my conscious mind soon overwhelms my subconscious guilt-trips, and I relax from any idea that what I am doing to women is wrong. They need me just as much as I need them.

I use my cell phone to call Marlee. It is essential that a man call a newly conquered woman the next morning after the initial sexual experience. This reassures her that the fling was not what it really was. Marlee was glad to hear from me, and she apologized for letting things get a little out of control. "I am not like that," she explained.

Most woman refrain from having sex on the first few dates in an effort to show that they are not "slutty." Like a man really gives a damn. But a woman must prove to herself that she is not a slut. Most women would gladly have sex on the first date with a man that they are attracted to, but they have taught themselves that self-respect (whatever they think that means) is more important than self-gratification. They feel better about themselves if they wait a few dates before going too far. All they are really doing is procrastinating.

Whether a man fucks a woman on the first date or the tenth date, if there is not going to be a connection and commitment, there will never be one. All a woman is doing by waiting is buying herself a few more dinners and free movies, receiving the attention she needs, and wasting more of her time. In reality, she is setting herself up to fall in love with this gentle man that will wait ten dates to screw her, and then dump her because she sucks in bed.

"Oh, you Gorgeous Thing," I respond sweetly. "It is I that needs to apologize for wanting you so bad. I haven't had a woman in such a long time, I couldn't help myself," I continued with sincerity.

I continued to stroke the inner chords of reassurance that are strung on the harp of a woman's heart. Each note played brought a smile to her face and a calmness to her soul. For 5 minutes on a cell phone she listened to harpsichordial melodies that convinced her that I was real. We set a date to meet again, and I ended the conversation making her believe she was the only one. I knew I was the only one—I planned it that way.

Before arriving at my office, I called Victoria's work and left a message on her voice mail that reassured her that she was the only one I would ever want to have sex with. I praised the softness and womanliness of her body and the way it makes me feel when we are together. In other words, I was saying that her body is pretty flabby, but I will overlook that fact because of her lips.

Women are constantly fishing or at least expecting some kind of compliment from their man about their appearance. Men are the biggest liars in this area. And why do we lie? Because we won't get any sex if we tell the truth. All women have to do is look at the swimsuit issue of Sports Illustrated magazine, one of the most popular among men, and they will see what their husbands and boyfriends think is sexy. Anything other than that Ladies, is not sexy. Sorry!

Sure we love you and will lie to you that we are not like other men and that you have always been the most beautiful woman in our lives. We'll sincerely admit that we are totally satisfied with the sexy lingerie that you often dawn to attempt to mimic a two-dimensional diva. Sure, we'll close our eyes as we make love to you and imagine that we are fucking the gorgeous babe we just closed up in one of our favorite magazines. But the fact is, we are men. We like hard, smartly formed bodies that get us excited. But, since most of us will never have the pleasure of unleashing our fantasies on a gorgeous body, we are happy to accept sex any way we can get it. Fat rolls, mushy butt and all. But we love you, Honey! You have always told us that lust is not love. And you were right!

From the description of the three women who I am currently in a relationship with, one would quickly realize that not much has been said about their beauty. Each has the best a woman has to offer in the erotic zones of her body, but none is ravishingly beautiful. Beautiful women are very hard to play. They get a lot of attention from all kinds of men, and are very particular with the kind of men that they allow in their bed. Nevertheless, these divas are not impossible to catch. A lot of men are too intimidated to approach or play them, not wanting to be turned down. A master Player has no qualms about playing a beautiful woman. However, he will soon realize that beautiful women are not near as passionate, and not near as sexual as their presence suggests. The worst lovers I have ever been with have been the most beautiful of all my conquests.

More homely women with the great bodies are better lovers than their more beautiful competitors. These women usually keep themselves in shape in hopes that they will land a man that is in the same kind of shape as they are. They probably were late bloomers when they were young, and were not used to the attention that men gave to more stunning women. Yet in the bedroom, they outshine popularly gorgeous women without question.

By far, the best lovers a man could ask for are the ugly ones that keep their bodies in tiptop condition. These realize that their faces would be better viewed behind a paper sack, so they turn all their attention to creating the best body they can possibly produce. When they have the body, they learn how to use it and they use it well.

Amy is by far the least attractive of any of my current women, and she is by far the most sexual in bed. Victoria is quite pretty and knows it, but has let her body suffer a bit in spite of her gorgeous lips. Marlee, though not as pretty as Victoria, has the type of breasts that will continually entice any man to want her even if she wore no makeup at all. Marlee has demonstrated a potential for extreme passion, and if that filly is ridden properly, she will prove to be a racehorse that any owner would be proud to run. If her breasts outlast anything else about her, a man will always want her.

During the 6 months of knowing Victoria, I was introduced to her religious beliefs and desire to find the "right man." I'm getting a little bored with playing her and making her believe that it just might be possible that I am he. Because I am the only one she is having sex with, she takes each of our sexual experiences as emotional bonding moments, which assure her with each orgasm that I am the "right one." I have sex with other women and find my time with them beginning to be more exciting and pleasurable than sex with her. This is the first of a few signs that let a Player know it is time to move on to something new.

Another sure sign of the need to broaden one's horizons is the presumptuous commitment agreement. With all women, a Player makes the first move towards a commitment in his relationship with her. This commitment is usually made right after the first session of intercourse when the woman is snuggling close and her heart is freshly served. The commitment is a simple one that demonstrates the man's ability to commit and his desire to have a continuing relationship with the woman.

"By making love to you, you do realize that I am committing to not having sex with anyone else but you as long as we're sleeping together," the Player faithfully proclaims. "It doesn't mean that we need to stop seeing other people, which would probably be wise to do so that we know that we are truly right for each other, but it does mean that we need to let the other know if we decide to sleep with someone else."

"Even if you choose to sleep with someone else besides me, that doesn't mean that I won't sleep with you; it just means that I would like the choice to do so or not," the Player continues his manipulation. "You do realize that everyone you sleep with, I have to sleep with too."

This charming lie prepares the woman to remain faithful to the man. He brought up the commitment thing in the first place. And he also was honest enough to say that even though he wasn't outrightly committing himself to be her man, he has shown that he respects the relationship enough to care about the well-being and emotional thoughts of his partner. The bullshit works wonders to assure women that your motives are pure.

When the woman brings up commitment, she is not bullshitting. She wants to know that she has her man and he will be only hers. She'll want to talk about the future and what the man sees in it for their relationship. This is the time the Player plans a different future.

"I am so glad God saw fit that we should meet," Victoria smiled one evening as we lay in her bed. "I am so lucky to have met a man like you. What do you think the future holds for us?"

My heart clenched up and I felt the deep anxiety arise from within my soul. I wanted to find a red light like the one used in the movie Men In Black, have her look into it, push the erase button, and erase every memory she had of me up to that moment.

"I love you, Honey," my mother whispered into my ear late one night. I felt her wet face on my forehead as she leaned over my bed and kissed me goodbye. She thought I was asleep.

"No matter where Mommy goes, you will always be in my heart. Goodbye!"

"No, Mommy," I cried and reached out and grabbed her to keep her from going. My tiny hands caught her coat and held on tight. My heart was clenched up, and this was the first time I felt the anxiety surface from deep within my soul. My mother was leaving me. I didn't understand why. I didn't care why.

She pried my tiny hands off of her coat and held me close for the last time. My sobs grew louder and she quieted them in her breast, trying to keep me from waking my other brothers asleep in the room. She held me for a long time rocking me and crying. I felt her tears wet my hair and her kisses never seemed to stop. I knew that I could keep her from leaving. She was my mother and she made a commitment to be my mother when she brought me into this world. I was her little boy. How could she leave me?

I must have fallen asleep again in her arms, because the next morning I woke up and she was gone. I ran all over the house looking for her. My father tried to calm me down, but I ran from him. My other brothers called me a baby and said that I should grow up. I didn't want to grow up. I wanted to be that little boy wrapped in his mother's arms forever. But she was gone, and her little boy then lost his innocence and respect towards all other women whom he should have been able to trust.

No one could erase those memories by using some ridiculous red light, and I knew I couldn't do anything about Victoria's memories of me. I knew it wouldn't be long before I left her hurting and longing for me as that little boy longed for his mother.

The Divorcee

No woman is played as easily as a recently divorced woman. They have usually ended a marriage that they believe has wasted many years of their lives. With their new freedom, they are looking to cover up the past and get on with the future. Being single offers them a new plate of men to choose from. They believe they have learned the important lessons from their ex-husband that will assure them that they will not make the same mistake twice in their selection of a mate. In this belief lies the opportunity a Player needs to make many kills among the herds of divorced women that are saturating the singles' scene.

A divorced woman does not necessarily look for the things a man should do, but more of the things that he shouldn't do. She remembers the time when she fell in love with her husband, how he swept her off her feet and acted like the man of her dreams. Yet after just a few short years of captivity—the Player's term for marriage—she found that she had married the man of her nightmares. Everything that the man did to create the nightmare is fresh in her memory, and stands in front of the remembrance of what he did to seduce her.

She looks for those nightmarish traits in the men she meets in the single world. She is astonished that she cannot find very many men that remind her of her evil husband. But, if she looks close enough, which she usually doesn't, she will find that almost all of them have many of the same traits her husband had when he courted her. She then begins to convince herself that maybe she just got an apple that looked nice, but had a worm in it. She sees other men as pieces of fruit that she would love to bite into, hoping that she finds sweetness and juicy explosions of ecstasy instead of worms. She has herself convinced that she'll bite into the apple, check for a worm, and discard it if she finds one.

A Player has no worms. He presents an apple of exquisite taste and sweetness, unlike any she has bit into before. She'll lightly nibble at first, hoping that her tiny bites will enable her to eat longer before finding the worm that she expects. The nibbles turn into mouthfuls, and before long, she is devouring the apple, convinced that there is no possible way that this marvelous piece of fruit could be tarnished by an insect.

And she is right. The apple she is eating is not tarnished by any insect. However, she should have checked with other women who have eaten that type of apple. What she doesn't know is that this type of apple is soon eaten and gone, and once in her stomach, creates the runs like she never had them before. Crouching effortlessly on the toilet waiting for the anguish and pain to end, she curses herself to no end about rushing to consume an apple that caused her to shit so much. The runs soon end and she feels better. "At least the apple didn't have any worms in it," she reasons.

Before long, all she can remember is how great the apple tasted in her mouth and she longs to eat another one. She soon gets used to the expected trip to the bathroom after the apple is digested, and her body soon dehydrates away into oblivion, which could have been avoided had she opted to eat a little protein—maybe a worm or two. But she sure liked those delicious apples.

A divorcee's sex drive is insatiable and needs very little prompting to become out of control. Obviously, sex wasn't too great during the last year of marriage, sometimes for many years, so she hasn't been emotionally turned on for quite some time. She's easily manipulated with simple brushes from a man passing, or even a passionate look can get her vagina pulsating.

After meeting Amy at the car wash the first time, we set up a time to meet at her house when the father of her two boys had them for the evening. Amy had been married to a controlling man who had been taught how to be a man by his father and taught how to love a woman by the same guy. If a boy is to properly learn how to love a woman, he must learn the lessons from a woman, and no other person is as well adapted to teach this than a boy's own mother. Amy's husband had a submissive mother who let her patriarch run the household and teach the curriculum. When Amy finally realized she had lost enough of her identity by trying to be what her husband wanted her to be instead of who she really was, she took her two boys and left.

Amy was ripe for the picking. Women who feel like they have lost many years of their lives trying to salvage a relationship, and that they lost themselves in the attempt, hit the singles' scene ready to move on and become who they really are. The problem is, at this point in their lives, they really don't know who they are. They follow a course of action that is necessary in order for them to be successful at becoming an individual again.

The only thing a divorcee can remember about being single is the things that she did when she was single the first time—play, play, show what you got, and date the best-looking guy you can find. The first night out as a new single woman is a little intimidating to a new divorcee. But it doesn't take her long to realize there are plenty of fish in the sea to choose from. If she has a nice body and is generally attractive, she will get all the attention she has ever wanted. Because she doesn't believe that she is ready for a serious relationship, she lets many guards down that allow men a perfect opportunity to play her.

Men that have been in the singles' scene for a long time learn how to present themselves in the best way possible to a divorcee. Their "strutting" becomes so natural that to a new woman on the scene, these men appear real and sincere. It's amazing to newly divorced women how many men are out there that are nothing like their controlling husband was. All of the sudden these women are being wined and dined—showed the attention that they felt they deserved, but didn't get from their husband. Most of the men they meet become everything they ever wanted.

Men can smell a newly divorced woman a mile away. We know that these women are used to having sex when they wanted and needed it, so we understand how easy it is to seduce them. We become a sympathetic ear that understands how hard it must have been for them to be treated that way by their malevolent husbands. "I would never treat you that way, if I had the opportunity and the pleasure of being your husband," we assure them. In other words, most divorced men know what kind of slime ball husbands they were when they were married, and simply imagine that the woman they are trying to seduce will be the one that changes their natures.

"I can't believe a man would ever yell at or hit a woman," we say surprised. We simply say everything that we knew our wives wanted us to say. But being single men we don't have to live up to it.

Players are men, but they don't play the same game as regular men. Good players understand the ways that other men use to attempt a seduction, and they avoid these orthodox techniques. Divorced women might be gullible and vulnerable, but they are not stupid. They quickly learn over time the games that men play and the lies that men use to convince them to have sex. Players catch women off guard and use the woman's lack of emotional balance to confuse her. The confusion is not seen as confusion, but rather as intrigue, by the woman being played by a Master.

"It is true," we begin, "that all men want is sex; and we usually do what we know we must do to get it."

"Finally a man that is honest," the woman thinks.

"I am not different than most other men biologically, but I have found that it does not serve my interest in happiness to engage in sexual activity too soon and ruin the opportunity of perhaps finding a good friend."

"Finally a man that just wants to be friends," the woman gets excited.

"I haven't had the opportunity to express my biological urges in quite a long time, but have formed some very valuable friendships with a lot of the women I have met. Sometimes it is hard on my female friends when our relationship does not progress beyond great conversation, fun activities, and deep feeling, but they understand that I do not want to make a mistake again."

"Finally a man that cares more about the woman than himself," the woman thinks, as her vagina gets wet.

"My ex-wife is a great person, and I am sure that I contributed to our divorce. I'm glad that we can still be friends, and I hope that she finds what she is looking for and that she, more importantly, finds happiness. I guess we didn't take the time to nurture a friendship when we first met, and I let the biological man overpower the need that I had for a best friend."

By this time, the woman is so enthralled with the illusion that the Player is everything she ever wanted in a man, that she finds herself having wet dreams about a man that she hasn't even dated. It's the illusion of the "right man" that gets women intrigued. The illusion has to be presented as a reality, with sincerity and consistency. A good Player does not have to make the first move towards physical intimacy. The entranced woman will jump his bones.

I met Amy at her house around 7 PM. She had invited me over to dinner and then to watch a movie. Her house was very clean and in immaculate order. There were candles lit in strategic places around her house that I am sure she had placed in order to create a more romantic ambiance than a single mother's palace offers. She was wearing very tight white pants, which held her firm butt exactly where any man would want it held—high and symmetrical.

It was quite obvious to me that she had already had dreamy sex with the man that saved her son, washed her car, and had a great looking body.

The first thing to do when entering a single mother's home is to compliment her extraordinary ability to make it as a single mother. Men can never over-compliment a woman. Women like to hear that they are acceptable and above the standard for a typical woman. Feeling special is the first step in foreplay. With a "this guy thinks I am special" attitude, a woman is ready to be charmed.

I poured on the accolades as Amy gave me a requested tour of her home. I showed more interest in her son's bedrooms than I did in hers. Hers was dimly lit, fresh smelling, had flowers on the nightstand, a 25" TV/VCR combo, and a perfectly made, queen size bed. Five minutes later, I couldn't even remember what was in the kid's rooms. I knew it wouldn't be too long before I was lying in that bed with Amy's gorgeous naked ass lying parallel to mine and enjoying a movie that I could care less about—a chick flick preferably.

"Finally I found a man that likes chick flicks," she swoons to herself.

We sat down to dinner and enjoyed some casual conversation about her kids and the joy they bring to her life. The conversation was garnished with made-up joyous experiences of my own days as a small boy. Each related anecdote brought a laugh from Amy and a twinkle from my eye. I was excellent at relating humorous incidents from my childhood—ones I imagined, but never experienced.

I took experiences that could have been funny and made them so. Often, I would really believe that my stories were as funny and as real as I presented them, and I would bond with the character of each story—the little boy that I imagined to be me. Each story was fabricated to please a mother. Each one a subconscious reality of what might have been had I enjoyed the presence of a real mom. I placed the little boy on a stage and made him do things that any mother would laugh at. The scenes were written to play on a mother's emotions—feelings that would endear her to a son. They came from somewhere deep within my subconscious, somewhere void and transparent—somewhere I'd rather forget.

We finished dinner and I graciously began to clear the table and put the dirty dishes in the sink.

"Finally a man that helps with the housework."

Amy told me to leave the dishes, took my hand, and led me into the living room to the cabinet that held her videos. I scanned over her videos until I came to a chick flick that I knew she had seen before.

The choice of a video is important. If she has seen the video before, she is more than likely going to be more interested in how good our bodies feel together than in the plot of the movie she has already seen. The video should contain more emotional scenes of passion than it does physical ones. Woman certainly get turned on with physical scenes of passion, but to get into her heart, which is a speed gate into her pants, an emotional scene is better.

After making our selection, Amy put in the video and I sat on the couch.

"Do you mind if I take off my shoes to be more comfortable?" I courteously inquired.

"Sure. Do whatever you must to be comfortable, please!" she responded.

"I don't think you want my naked body sprawled all over your couch on our first date, now do you?" I shot back with an ambiguous question. The question was supposed to be humorous, but was filled with an innuendo of truth to see just how close I was to getting into her pants that night.

"I'm not sure that would be such a bad sight," she laughingly remarked.

She didn't see my smile as I bent down and took off my shoes.

Women like to be touched. Most men use the orthodox, "Can I massage your shoulders?" facade to get their first touch of a woman's body. A player explains his interest in snuggling and holding someone close. I usually explain how wonderful it felt as a little boy when my mother used to snuggle with me—which was one of the few truths I play with—and how I enjoyed snuggling with some of my female friends in a very platonic way, of course.

Amy, like most women, didn't have a problem with snuggling. I asked her what her favorite position was and she gave the generic response that she loves them all. I suggested spooning (the preemptive phase to "forking"). Spooning is the most advantageous for the man. Spooning is when the man lies on his side, preferably the side of the hand he uses the least, and the woman snuggles her body into his, kind of like putting two spoons together. In this position, not only can the man feel his penis nestled gently between the cheeks of her butt, but his most coordinated hand is free and ready to prepare the filet.

The woman should be held snugly, but not too tight. She should be able to feel your muscles flex each time you move to make position adjustment or caress her. Once the movie is going and she has pushed her body into position, the first sound out of your mouth has to be, "Ahhhhhh, this feels nice." Not "good," but "nice." Most women are not going to slam their body into you and show any initial interest that she loves the feel of your dick on her ass. Subtle slow pressure up against her back will tell you if she is responsive. If you push too hard at first, she will take it as you being uncomfortable and might move away a bit for your sake. A responsive woman will slightly push backwards telling you that she likes what she feels. And she will usually respond with, "Mmmmmmm, yes it does."

All good filets are prepared properly by removing the bony spine. In the case of a woman, her spine must become putty in a man's hands. This means that her nervous system must come under the control of his touch. This is accomplished by caressing. Usually the less coordinated hand is placed near the top of the woman's head. Her head should be gently resting on your bicep. In this position, it is important that your flexes during muscle enticement (an easy way to explain showing off your muscles in subtle ways) do not bounce her head too high. This is annoying, and a sure sign to her that you're thinking about your own muscles instead of her comfort.

Amy's soft hair flowed over my hand. She had indicated that she was very comfortable with the position we were in by moving her hips gently backward with each tiny push I signaled. Her butt was so fine. It was hard for me to keep my erection in check and from showing a lack of self-control. I begin to caress the top of her head, softly whispering, "I hope that's not a bother to you, I sure love your hair."

"I love to be touched," she responded.

I could feel her nerves come under my control. My free hand, which just so happened to be my most coordinated one, began to massage her arm. I began at her shoulder and slowly moved down her arm until I reached her wrist. She turned her hand upward letting me know that she was enjoying what I was doing. I softly tickled her wrist for a moment then moved to her hands, which I massaged deeply and purposefully.

At this point, she was almost under my control. A human being can be hypnotized with the appropriate touches. Women who have been stroked just right, don't mind if a man's hand finds its way toward the breast area. They seem to be lulled away into a sense of comfort and security. In this state of ecstatic euphoria, any movement from a man seems sensible and natural. If a man is patient enough in caressing a woman, he will soon find that she will allow him to explore areas of her body that in any normal situation would seem inappropriate for someone she barely knows.

My free hand left Amy's arm and found her outer thigh region. I massaged it for a moment and moved down her leg as far as my arm would reach in that position. I could feel the strength of her thigh, and when I continued my hypnotic massage back up her leg, I found half of her buttocks in perfect position to be touched. Since she had on a pair of loose pants, I was able to feel the contour and firmness of her ass. God, I wanted her at that time. My control was wavering. I knew she wasn't prepared enough, so I brought myself back under control.

I subtly reached for the inside of her thigh. She adjusted her weight a bit and turned her hips slightly allowing me better access. She spread her legs slightly and moaned softly. I knew I had her. I proceeded to massage the inside of her thigh and stopped just shy of the soft transition area where her thigh meets her butt—just underneath the vagina area. I could feel the heat emanating from between her legs.

She was now turned almost entirely on her back. The massage had her mesmerized into erotic oblivion. The hand that was nearest her head began its strategic plan of getting her totally out of self-control into my complete control. It gently massaged the temple regions of her head and soon found the supple areas just under her chin.

The sure sign of what she wanted me to do to her would be shown in how she reacted to my fingers next to her lips. I felt the tip of my index finger to make sure that it was not callused or rough in any way. If I found it to be, I would serendipitously find the fingertip that was the softest. My index finger was fine, so it found her lower lip and passed on it flirtatiously. She immediately opened her mouth just a bit and let her wet tongue brush the next pass of my finger. With that invitation I put another finger on her lower lip and pushed both toward her tongue. Her head bent forward slightly and she gently licked both of my fingers. That's all I had to do. She grabbed my fingers in her hand and subconsciously treated them like a delicious lollipop that she hadn't eaten in ages. She was completely under my control.

My hand nearest her midsection began to caress her stomach area and soon found her erect nipples protruding through her blouse. Each time her nipple was touched, she would moan slightly and arch her hips. It was time to tenderize the filet and prepare it for the frying pan.

I slowly unbuckled her belt and played like it was difficult to undo the first button on her pants.

Now, for an expert who has undone hundreds of buttons just like Amy's, it really wasn't a problem. But for a master Player to know that the woman really wanted him, it was necessary to see just how much help she would offer in undoing her pants.

Amy's sucking became more profound and deep on my fingers. Her other hand worked its way toward her pants buttons and undid what I could have easily have undone myself. She didn't stop at the first button but undid all the remaining buttons, opened her pants as far as they would go, and grabbed my hand and put it where her fly flaps had covered. I took the hint, lifted up her panties with my fingers, and sought for the butter that was now sizzling in the pan.

Now every man knows that not all fillets taste or smell the same. Yet, he very well knows that if it doesn't smell like it should, his lips aren't going anywhere near it. Women seldom detect the subtle ways that men test their vaginal juices for cleanliness and palpability.

My middle finger found the moist upper area of Amy's vagina. She was extremely wet. Most men would agree, "the wetter, the better." I forced my hand down her pants as far as I could comfortably reach it and slid my middle finger slightly into her vagina. She stopped sucking on my fingers, arched her hips up, and moderately sighed. She could tell my hand was restricted by her pants and accommodated me by arching up as high as she could and used her free hand to lower her pants off her hips.

I pulled my hand out of her panties and helped her remove her pants and then her panties. Once her lower section was naked, she laid her body back on the couch. I brought my free hand up to her face and took her head in both my hands. At this point it was futile to attempt to seduce her with subtle kisses. She was already seduced. We passionately kissed, wetting each other uncontrollably with erotic drool. This was the strategic time that I could smell her on my fingers. My hand was clasped on the side of her head, my thumb on her cheek. I began to kiss the side of her face and was completely aware at this time that her smell was acceptable. It was a clean, natural smell, hardly noticeable. The fillet was perfect.

She grabbed my arm, arched her hips back and put my hand back to her vagina. I continued to tenderize her until I knew I had to put the filet in the frying pan before it disintegrated from the tenderizing mallet. Her hand found my crotch and she barely could constrain herself from pummeling it. She frantically grabbed at my belt and my pants button.

Amy was a divorced woman who hadn't felt this much passion in a long time. She was totally susceptible to anything I wanted to do to her. The old feelings of climax and orgasm beckoned her to remembrance. I wasn't a man that she loved; I was a man that she wanted. Her forced celibacy had caught up with her, and she fought its restrictions and limitations. She, like so many divorced women, wasn't thinking with her head, she was headed in her thinking. She was headed toward that passion that she had experienced in the past. She was headed toward the calming relaxation that a climax would bring her. She was headed toward heartbreak.

We ripped at each other's clothes until we were completely naked. I was yearning for her, but was totally surprised that her yearning was much more intense than mine. I was lying on my back on the couch and she pinned me down with ravishing lust. She straddled me with her incredibly strong legs and forced herself down on me. Because the pan was oiled and ready, that filet slid on with incredible ease. For the next 20 minutes I did nothing but watch that filet cook in its own fat. And when it was done cooking, I ate it eagerly.

I can't remember what that movie was about. Nor did I care.

Moving On

A Player never wants to be known as someone that uses women. When it is time to move on to another woman, it makes sense that he doesn't leave his conquests believing that they have been used—even though they have.

No doubt, they will be hurt, but if the bridge isn't burned, there is a chance that it might be usable again someday. A proficient Player has a never-ending stream of women coming in and out of his life; but he also has a substantial reservoir of what are called "inserts." Though rare, there are times when a Player doesn't have someone lined up for the evening or weekend. This is when "inserts" are necessary.

I called Victoria and told her I needed to speak with her after work that evening. I sounded a little morose and for a reason—she was soon to be out of my life. She seemed concerned and wondered what was wrong. She pressed for me to explain what I felt on the telephone. (This was exactly the reason why I used a morose tone of voice.) It's much easier for a man to dump a woman without personally facing her. Yet, to maintain his pseudo-integrity, a Player tries to convince the woman that he would rather talk to her in person. Of course, the woman wants to know what the problem is NOW! The nature of a woman creates her own dilemmas.

"I feel like I am losing the best thing that has ever happened to me," I sadly commenced my bullshit. "I don't think I can ever be to you what I have the potential of being, if I don't know who I am myself."

Ah, the "I've got to find myself" male excuse for "I am tired of you and want to move on." We play with a woman's inherent desire to succor and aid in healing, and hope that she can sense our need to heal. We don't need to find ourselves. We know exactly who we are. We just don't want our women to find out.

"I guess my inability to trust myself to a committed relationship is causing my anxiety. I thought that by loving you and allowing you to share my life I could somehow find the trust in myself that I need in order to be able to trust you," I continued.

"Does this mean that you don't want to continue to see me?" Victoria choked out.

"Absolutely not!" I immediately shot back. "I need you as a friend right now, and know if we can keep our relations platonic, you will be the friend I need at this time in my life."

Players say this because we know that a woman who has been sexually involved with us for a long period of time can never just be our friend. Women generally fall in love with a man who she is monogamous with. If a woman ignorantly agrees just to be a friend, the man can usually get one more session of sex out of her before he tells her that he can't see her again because the passion is too great. The woman can relate to this, and usually accepts the man with respect for giving up sex in order to find himself, improve himself, and make himself ready for a committed relationship.

Who's giving up sex? We're just giving up a woman we're tired of.

"Is there any way I can help you through this?" Victoria sincerely inquires.

"The best thing you can do for me is to just accept me as a friend. You probably deserve someone a lot better than I am anyway," I say, trying to sound pathetic.

Ah, the ol' "I am not good enough for you" bullshit. Of course we want the woman to retort the statement by telling us that she doesn't want anyone else, and that we have everything she will ever need in a man. What would stop a Player in his tracks is if the woman responded, "You are right, you're not good enough for me." It would crush his pathetic ego. But women don't. They are in love—codependent on the acceptance of a man.

"You have heard the statement," I continue, "If you love something, set it free. If it comes back to you, it was always yours. If it doesn't, it never was. Well, I have little doubt that you would be disappointed in letting me go for awhile. You and I both know there is no other like you."

A Player obviously came up with the "If you love…set it free…" idea. A perfect way to get off the hook looking like a truly compassionate man who loved his woman, but needed to go off and prove to himself that he is worthy of her love. Does a woman actually think that by "setting a man free" he will come running back to become "un-free" again? Get a grip, Ladies. The saying should be:

"If you love something, hang on to it. If it still wants to go, let it, because it didn't love you in the first place. And if you think it will come back to you, think again stupid."

I caught Victoria off guard in breaking up with her. She was at work, and didn't have much time to think about it. I knew she wanted to see me again and make sure that this is what I wanted.

"Just give me a few weeks alone to make sure I am making the right decision," I concluded.

She agreed to that, and that was that.

Two weeks had passed and Victoria called to see how I was doing. I didn't return her calls. After 5 attempts, she finally got the hint and never called again. I'll miss her lips, but I am ready to find her replacement. The fact is, the moment I ended my conversation with her, I started looking. I still had Marlee and Amy as regulars, so I wasn't pressed for immediate success.

I wondered how hard it was for my mother to move on with her life. Many times growing up I wondered if she missed me, or if she had forgotten about me. Does a mother's love for her son ever go away? Or was it hidden behind the shame she felt in leaving me and my siblings? I didn't think about it too much when I would leave a woman, but I did wonder how my mother would feel if she got dumped. Maybe it was my way of wanting her to hurt for me.

Moving on...to what? I was not moving on to anything. I was existing in a vacuum. No, more like a tornado. I would suck women into my life, tumble them around for a bit, and spit them out. Yet, I wasn't really moving on. I was just a swirling wind that seemed to thrive on destruction and power. What started the winds that caused the tornado? What would cause it to end? Questions I couldn't answer.

Questions I didn't want to answer. For if the winds ceased, who would I be?

That evening I stood in front of my full-length mirror analyzing my body as if I were a woman desiring it. I began to dance a little, pretending that I was the band and ensemble. My penis became a guitar and my hand held an invisible microphone. All men have done this before. It seems to be our way of lusting after ourselves.

Oh Lord it's hard to be humble
When you're perfect in every way.
I can't wait to look in the mirror
Cause I get better lookin' each day.
To know me is to love me
I must be a hell of a man.
Oh Lord, it's hard to be humble
But I'm doin' the best that I can!
I used to have a girlfriend
But I guess she just couldn't compete
With all of these love-starved women
Who keep clamoring at my feet.

I remembered these words to an old Mac Davis song, and sung them with a hopeless belief that they were true. I stopped the naked dance and stared at my twinkling eyes in the mirror. "Who the hell are you?"

I am a Player.

Epilogue

Crime—an act committed or omitted in violation of a law. Law—the rules of conduct established by the authority or custom of a society.

A Player's actions do not violate any established rule that society has acknowledged and accepted. Perhaps it's because society doesn't really know who to blame for his actions. Maybe society itself is to blame and therefore, it remains in denial; thus attempting to cover its own responsibility.

The relationship between a man and woman is changing drastically and rapidly. Marriage has become nothing more than an attempt by two parties to please the laws and traditions that society has antiquated. The traditional family unit is vanishing and becoming obsolete.

Society has perpetuated a norm for what it considers to be "beautiful" people. Women and men judge themselves by this norm. If they fail to meet this "norm," both sexes feel inadequate and abnormal. Each makes an attempt to somehow fulfill society's perception of what he or she should look like whether in real relationships or in fantasy.

A Player uses what society has created and takes advantage of its perceptions in order to make himself happy. A free society guarantees an individual the right to life, liberty, and the pursuit of happiness. Why should a Player's happiness be any less important than that of another?

But is he truly happy? Do his actions deceptively offer happiness to his victims, and then deny them the inalienable right to pursue it? True happiness and fulfillment only comes to he who finds it within himself. This book has presented the mind of a Player who found no lasting happiness in being one. However, he presented no viable solution to his dilemma. The question still remains: With how our society is currently structured, is there a solution?

Indeed, we are all "Players" of some kind or another in the game of life.

And by understanding the nature of a Player, we can better understand society. And since we are society, we can better understand ourselves. Understanding ourselves will enable us to transform the society we have created into a better place, and allow us to more successfully pursue the happiness that we all desire, without giving up our personal liberties and individuality. Here's to happiness.

—The Editor

CPSIA information can be obtained
at www.ICGtesting.com
Printed in the USA
FSOW02n1218121116
27166FS